TRUE IMAGE
S T U D I O S

COLOR THE US
FLAG EDITION

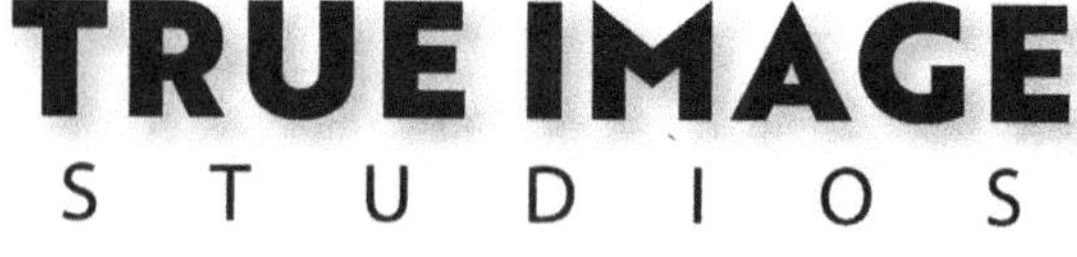

Copyright 2023
True Image Studios LLC.
trueistudios@gmail.com
ISBN 979-8-9865340-1-5

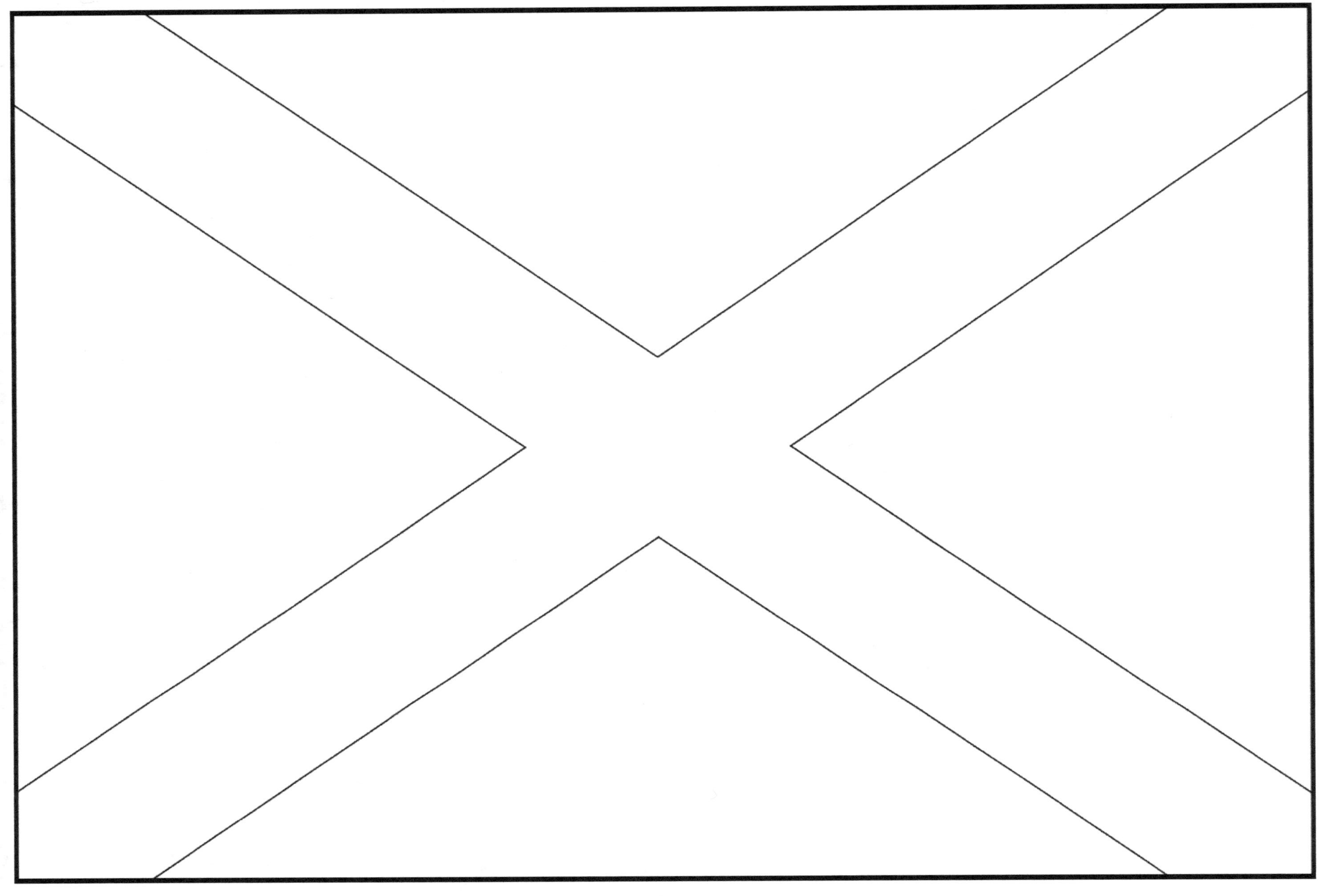

ALABAMA

THIS BOOK BELONGS TO:

____

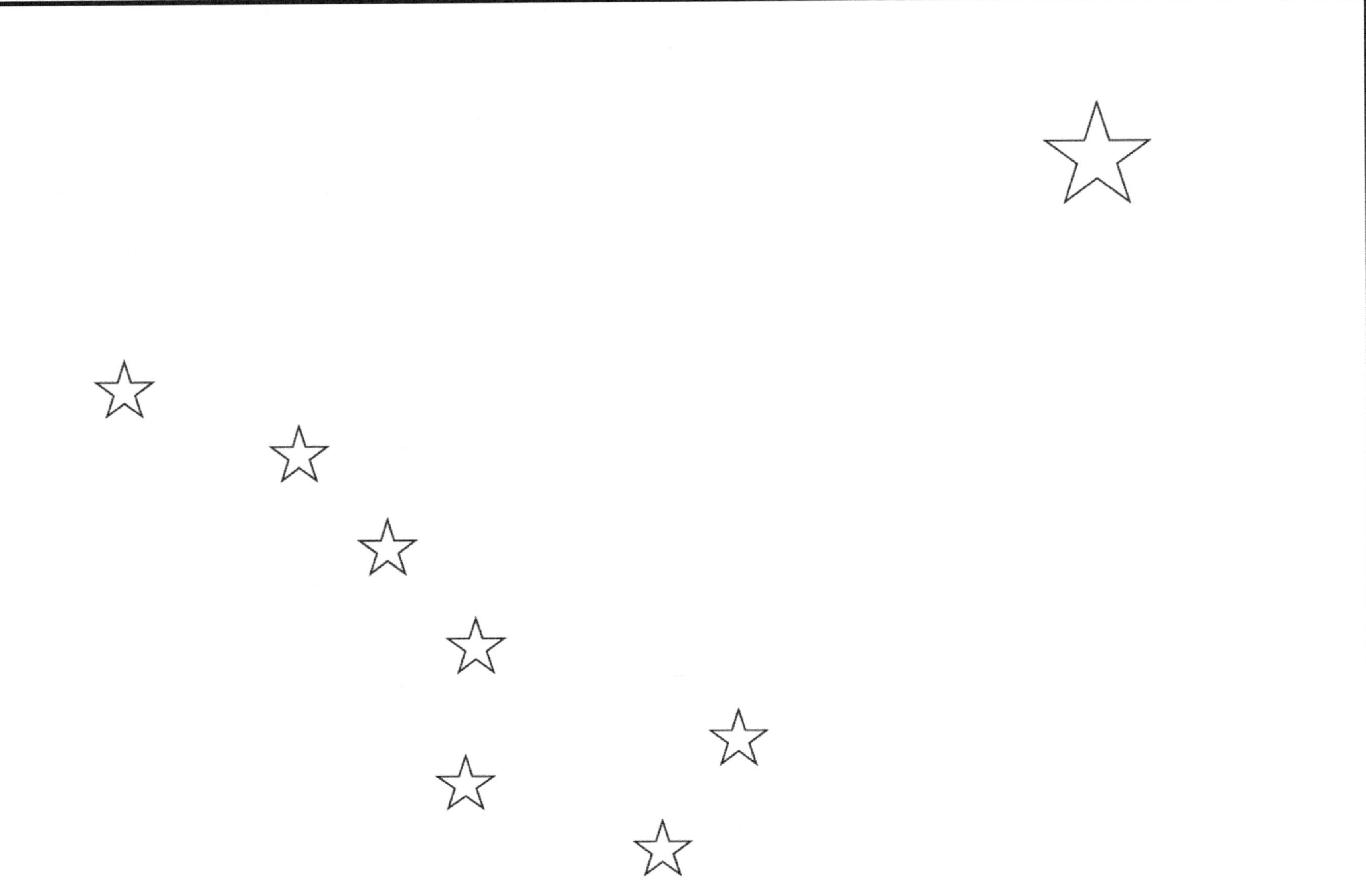

ALASKA

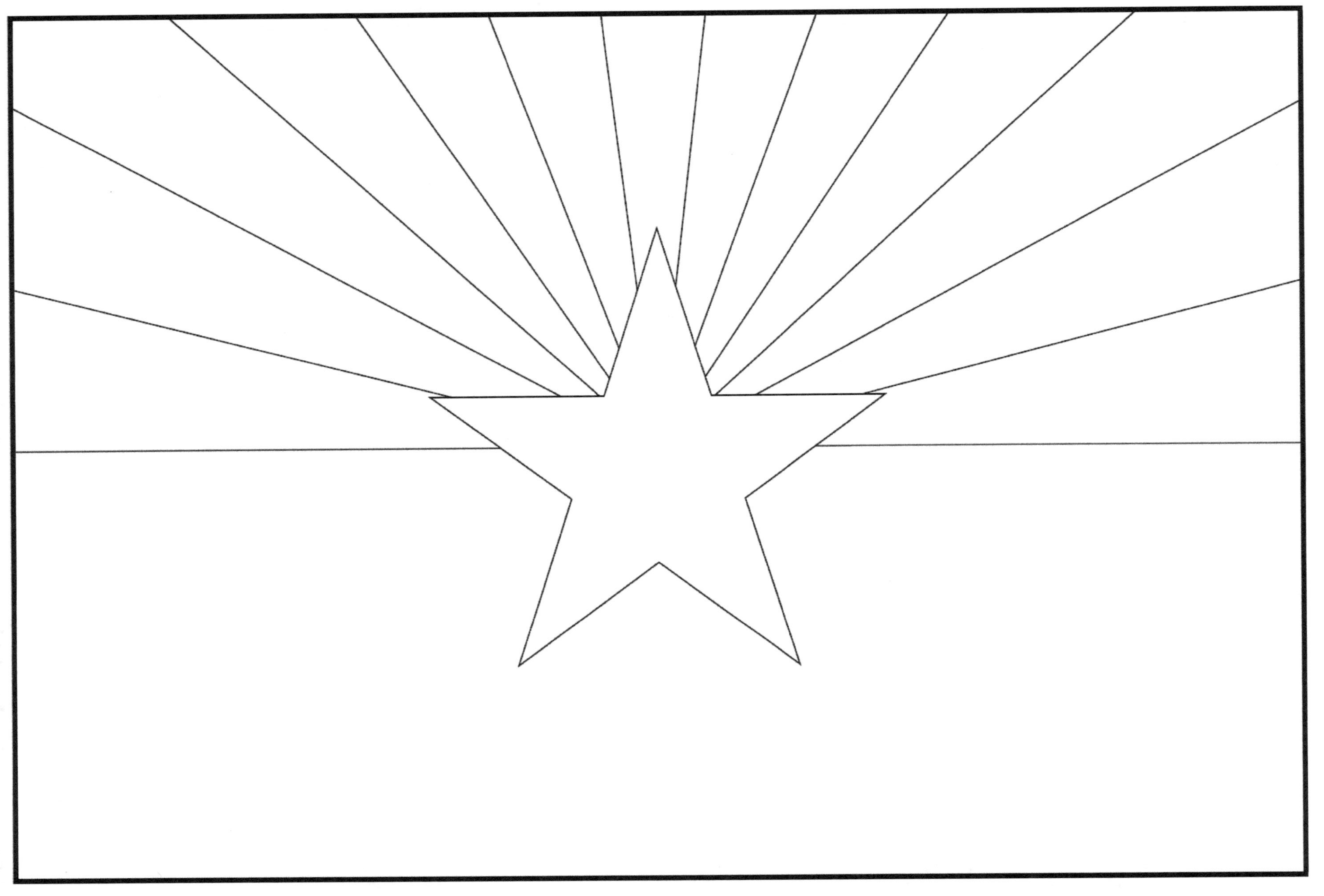

ARIZONA

  COLOR THE US: FLAG EDITION

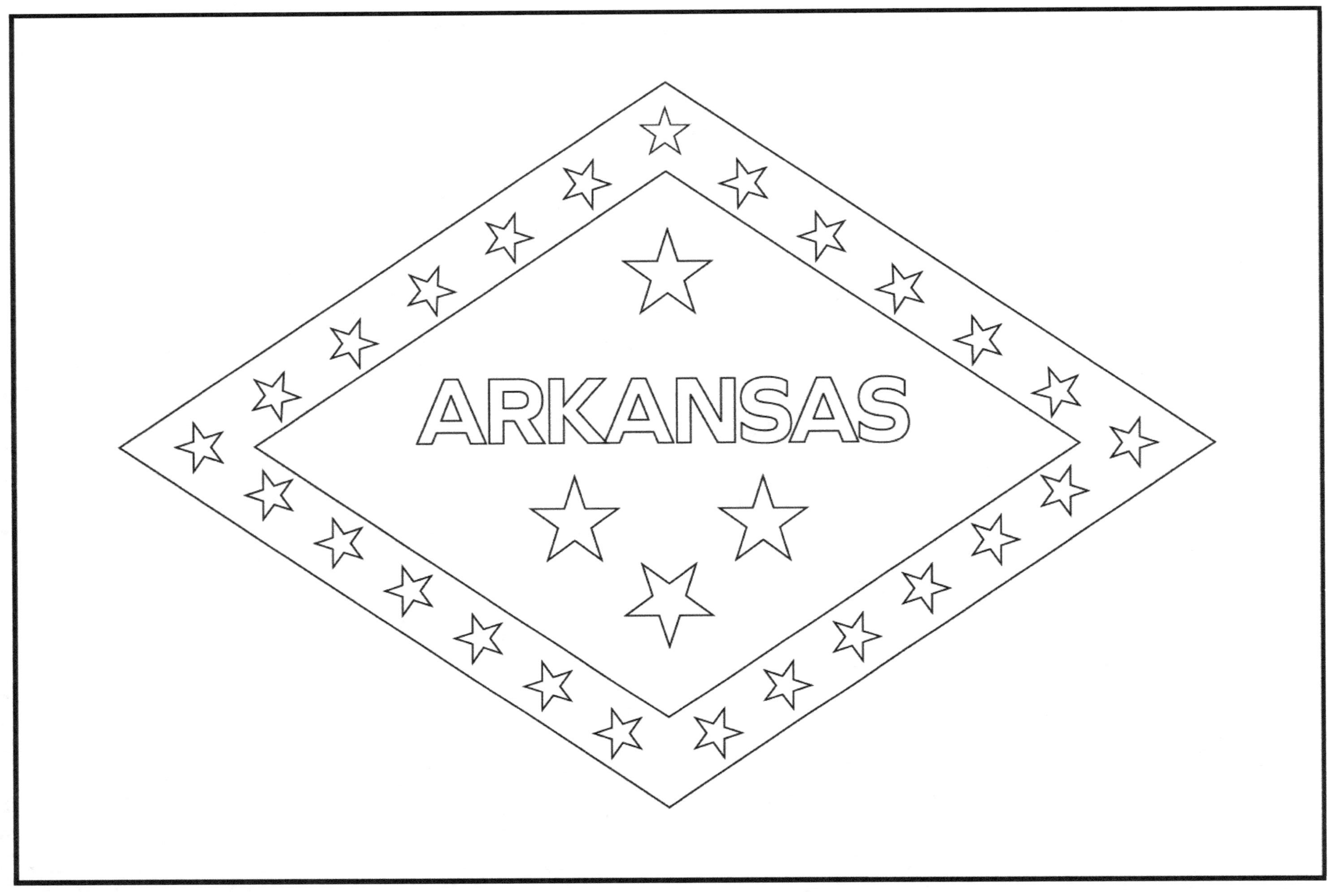

ARKANSAS

CALIFORNIA REPUBLIC

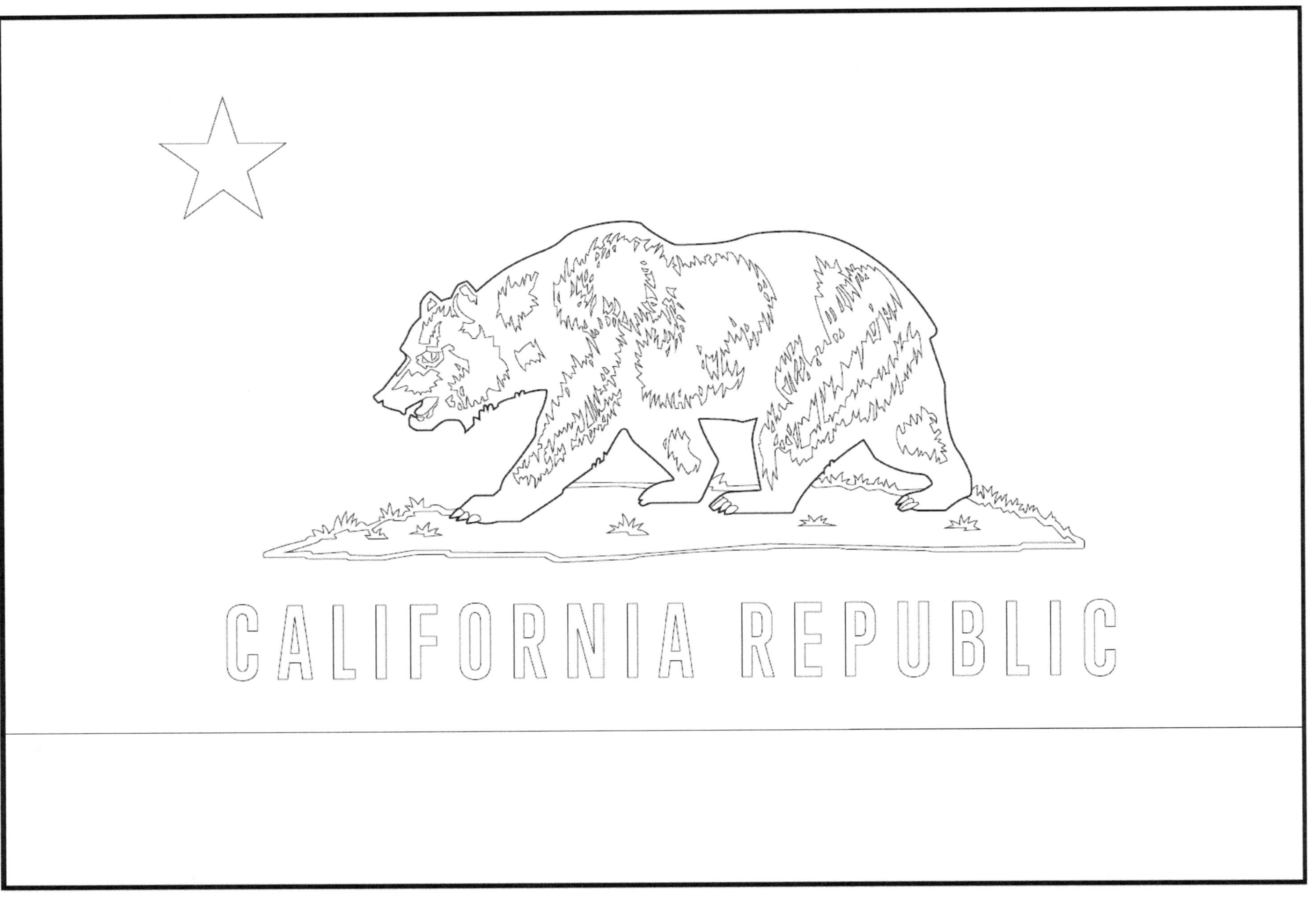

CALIFORNIA

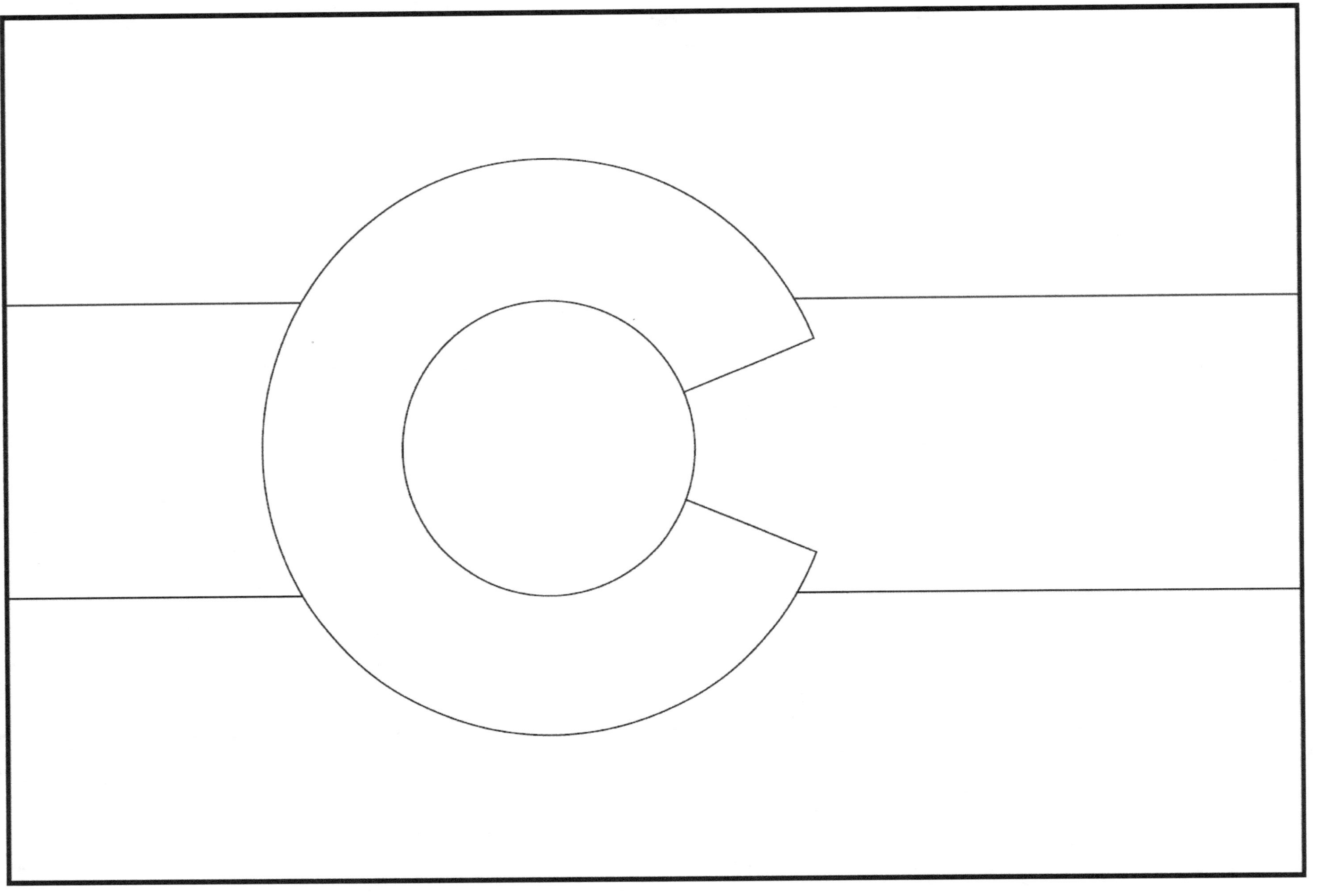

COLORADO

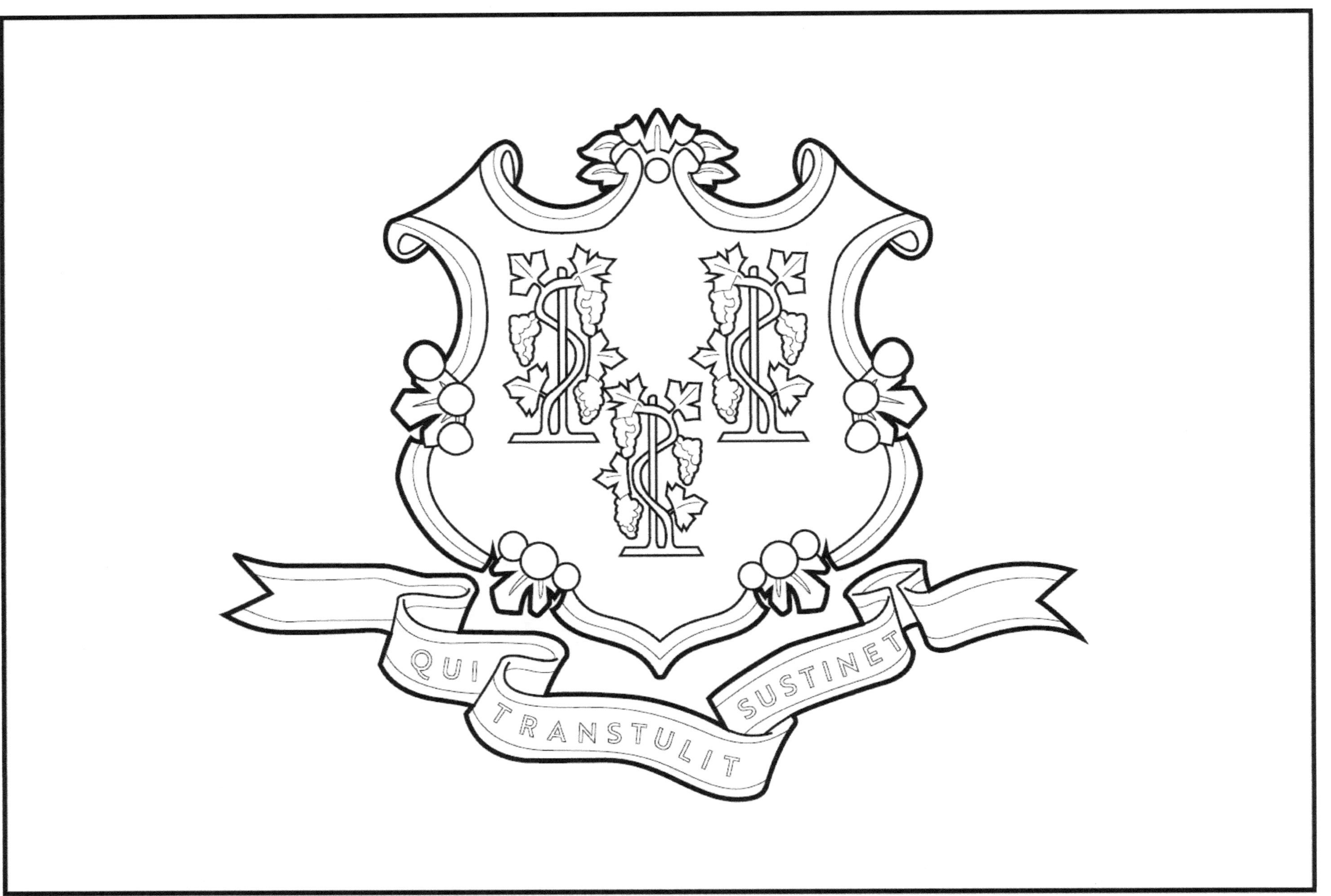

CONNECTICUT

  COLOR THE US: FLAG EDITION

LIBERTY AND INDEPENDENCE
DECEMBER 7, 1787

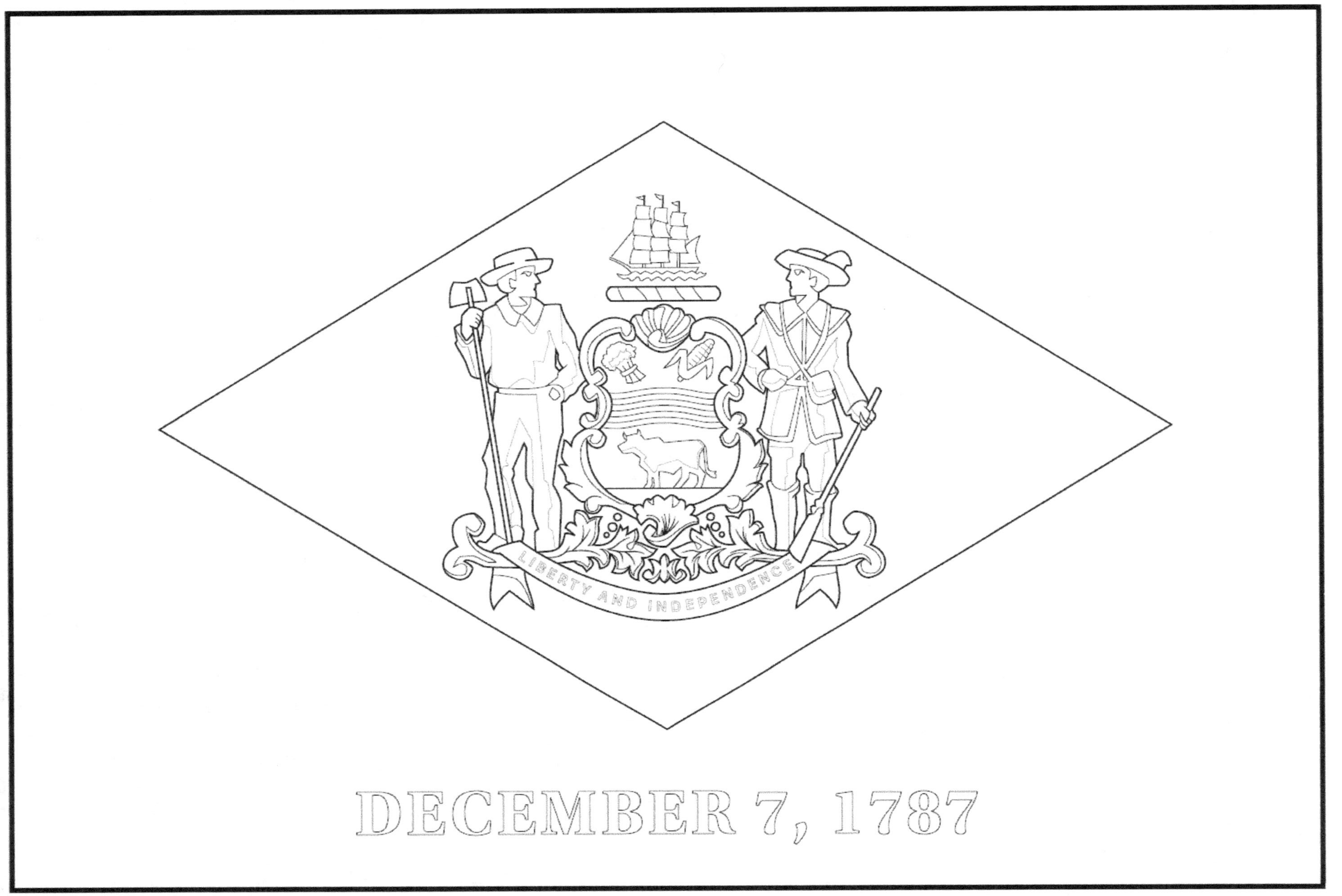

DELAWARE

GREAT SEAL OF THE STATE OF FLORIDA
IN GOD WE TRUST

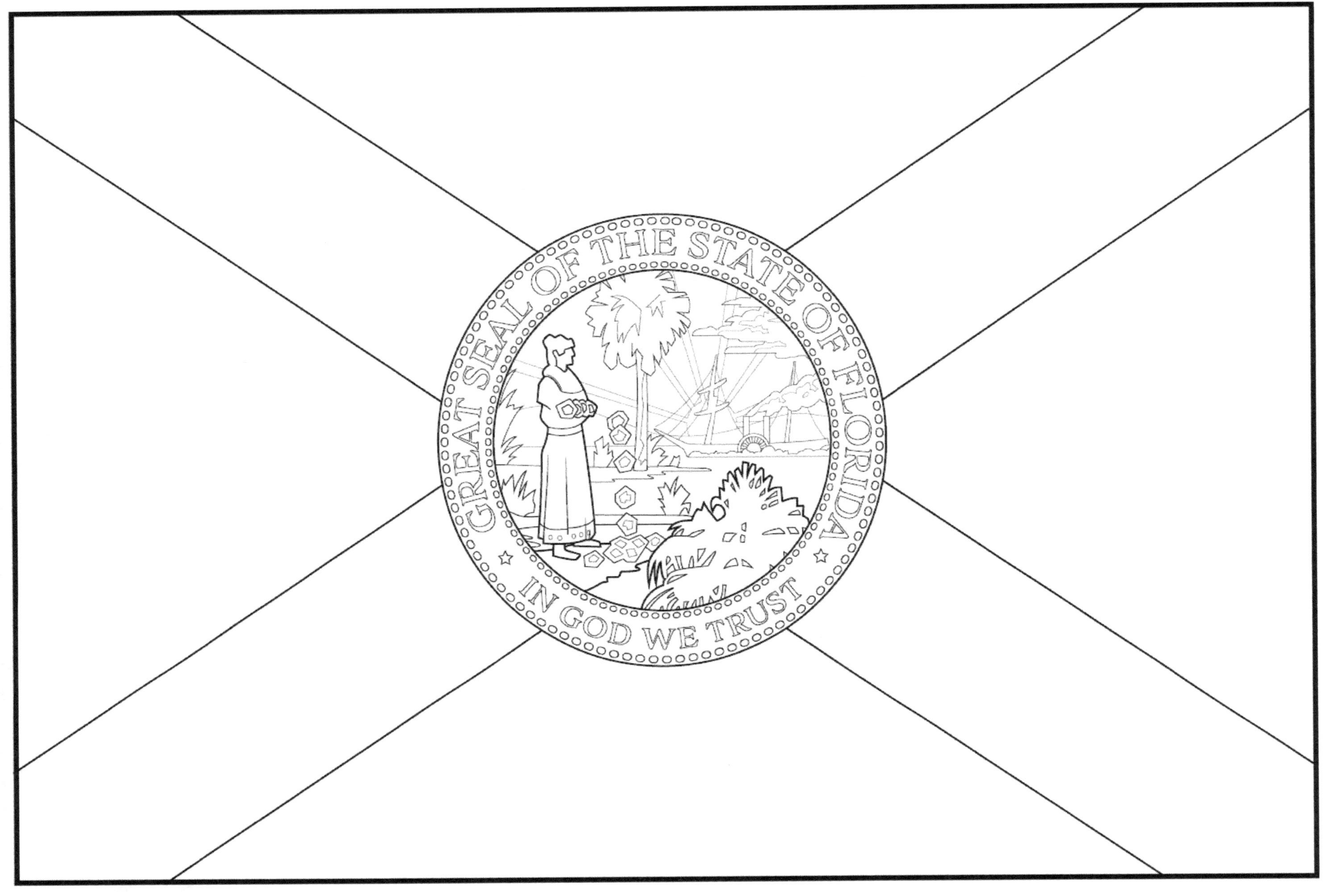

FLORIDA

CONSTITUTION
JUSTICE
WIS
DOM
MODER
ATION
IN GOD WE TRUST

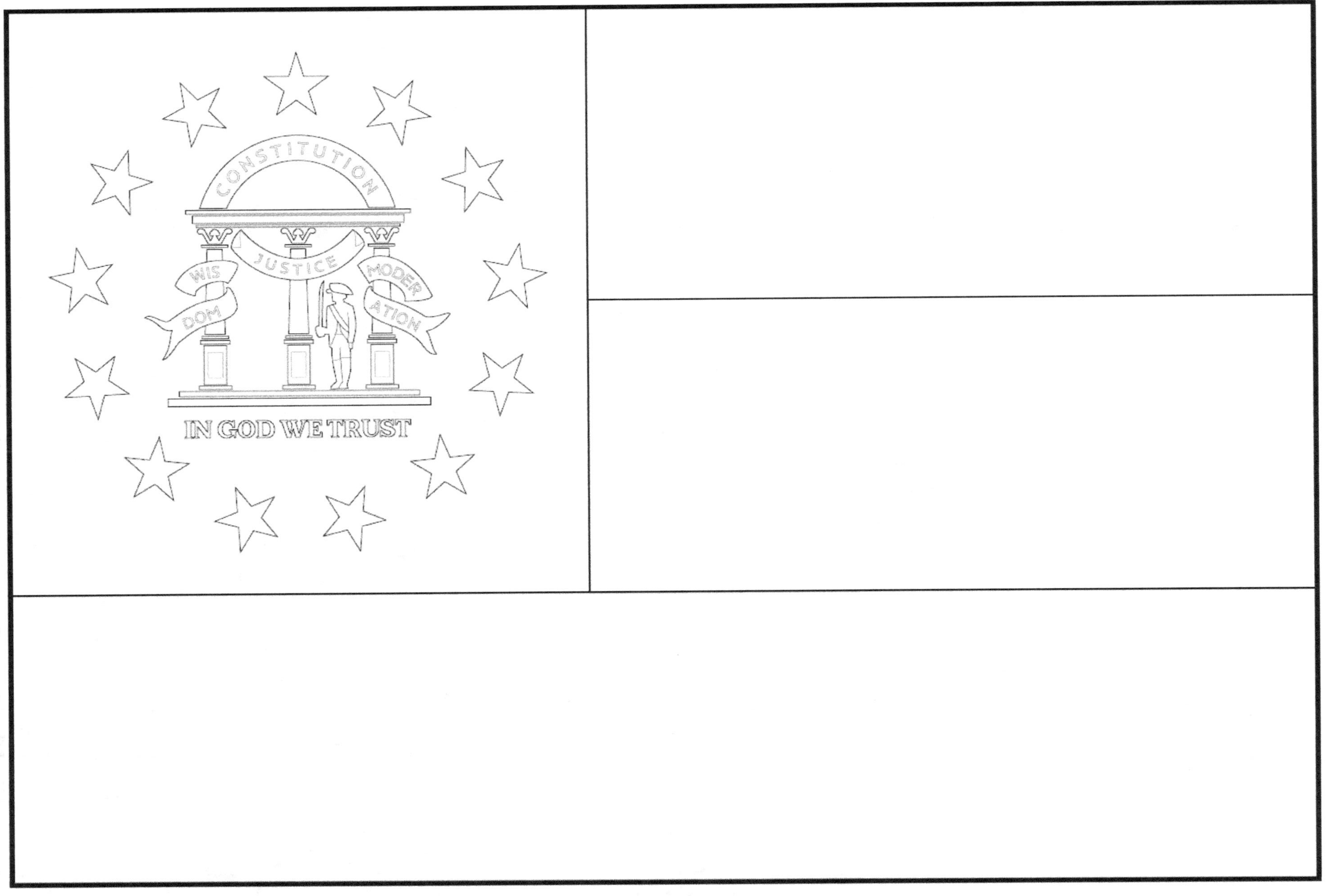

GEORGIA

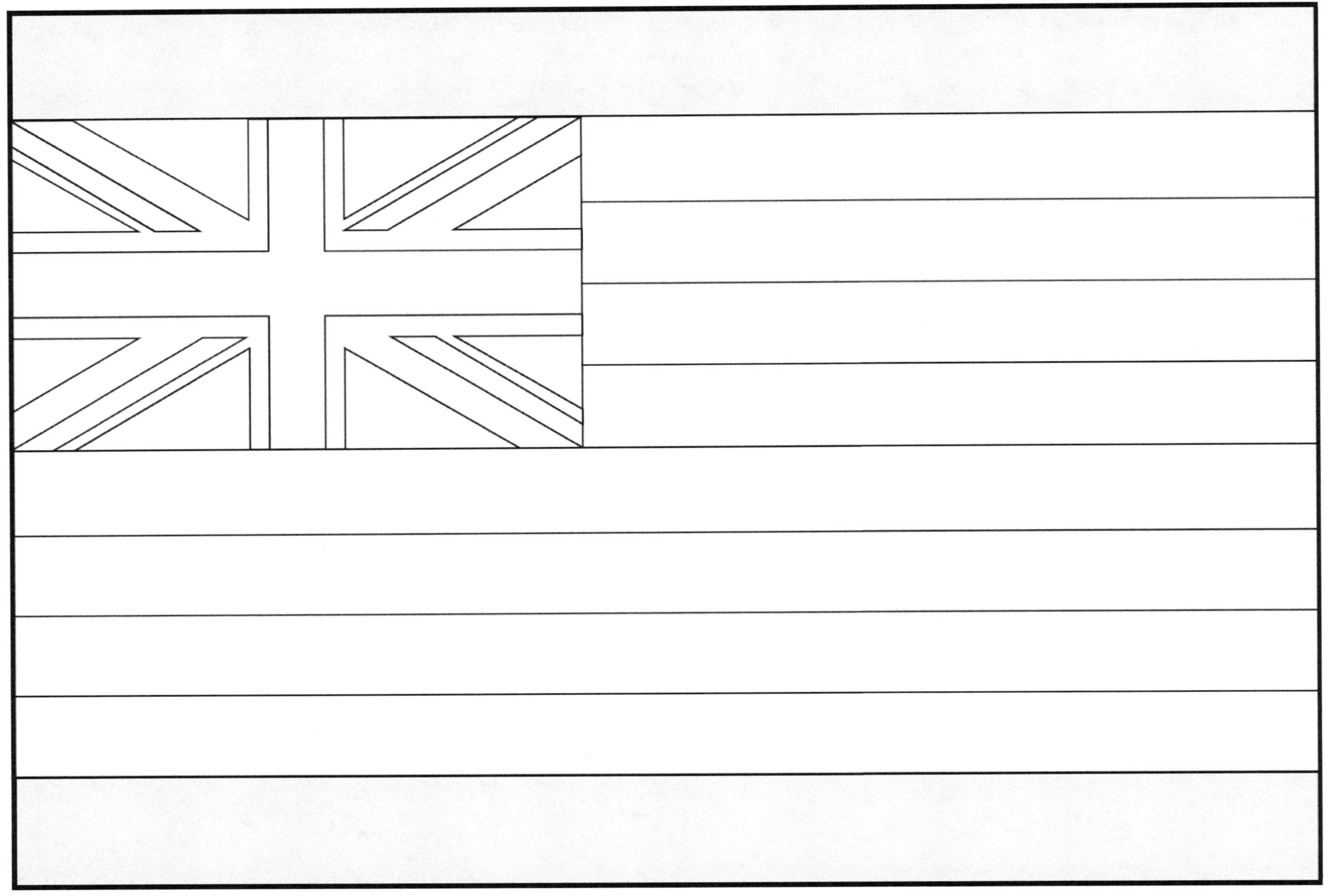

HAWAII

GREAT SEAL OF
ESTO PERPETUA
THE STATE OF IDAHO
STATE OF IDAHO

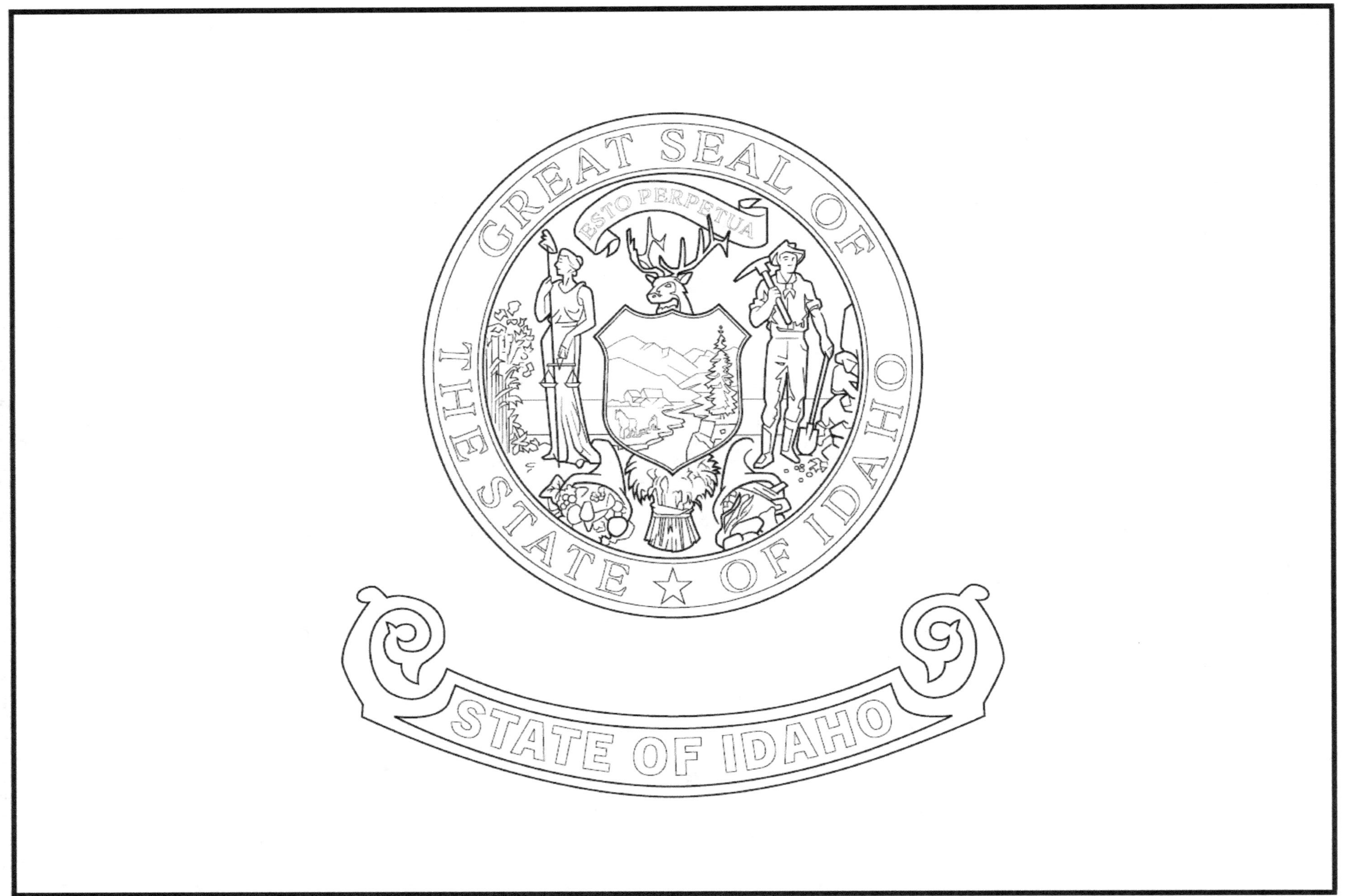

IDAHO

UNION
NATIONAL
SOVEREIGNTY
STATE
1868
1818
ILLINOIS

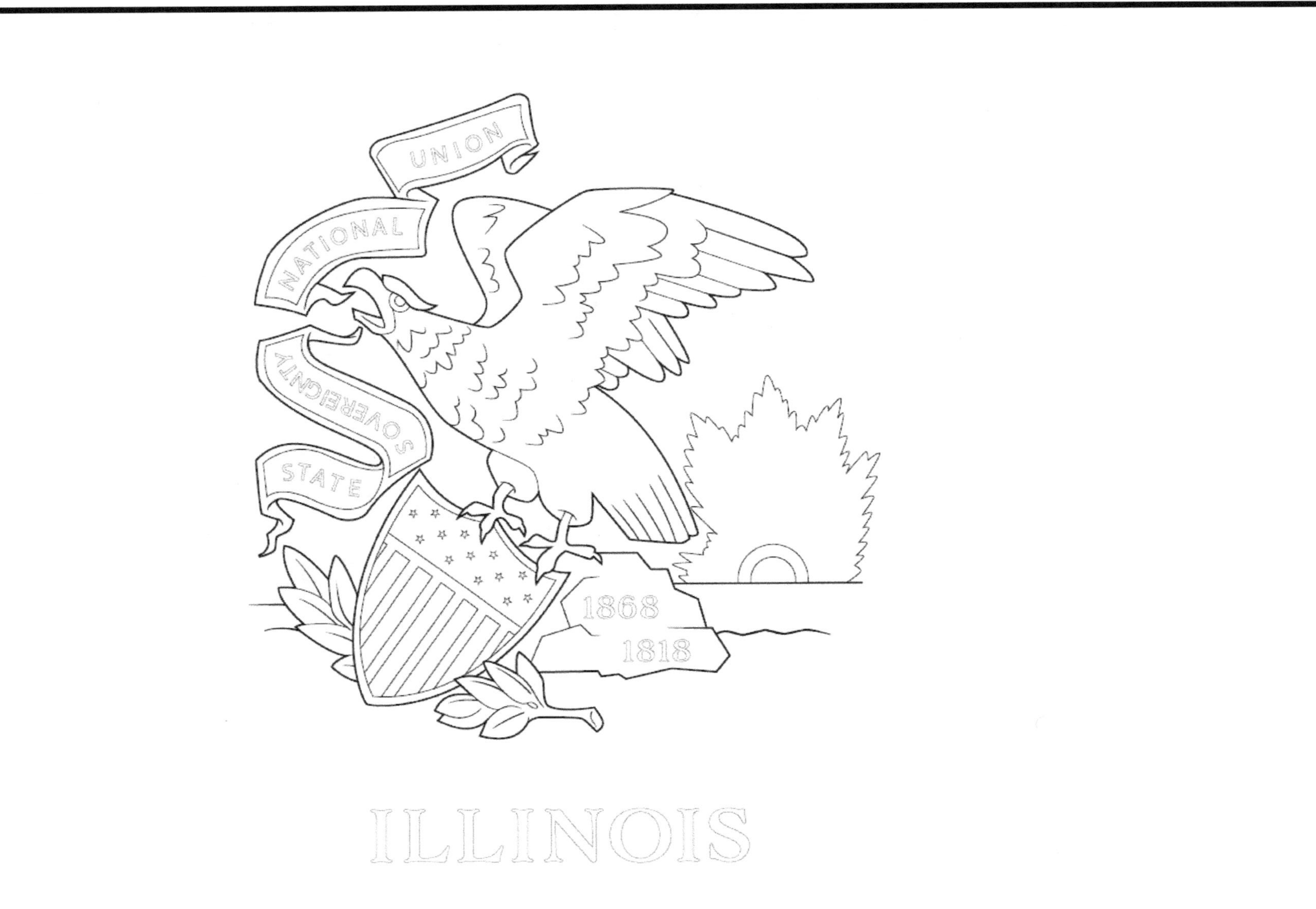

ILLINOIS

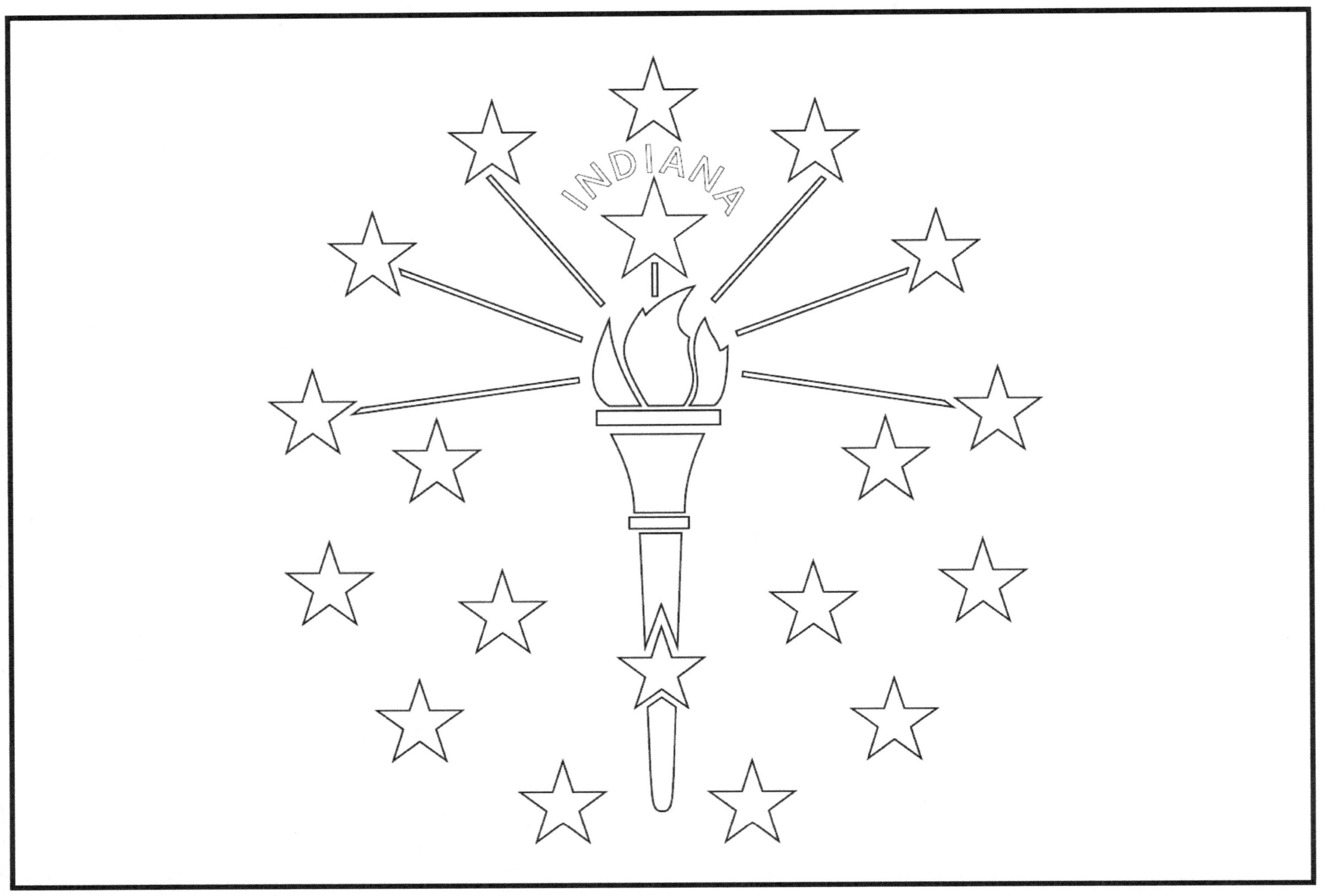

INDIANA

OUR
LIBERTIES
WE PRIZE
AND OUR
RIGHTS
WE WILL
MAINTAIN
IOWA

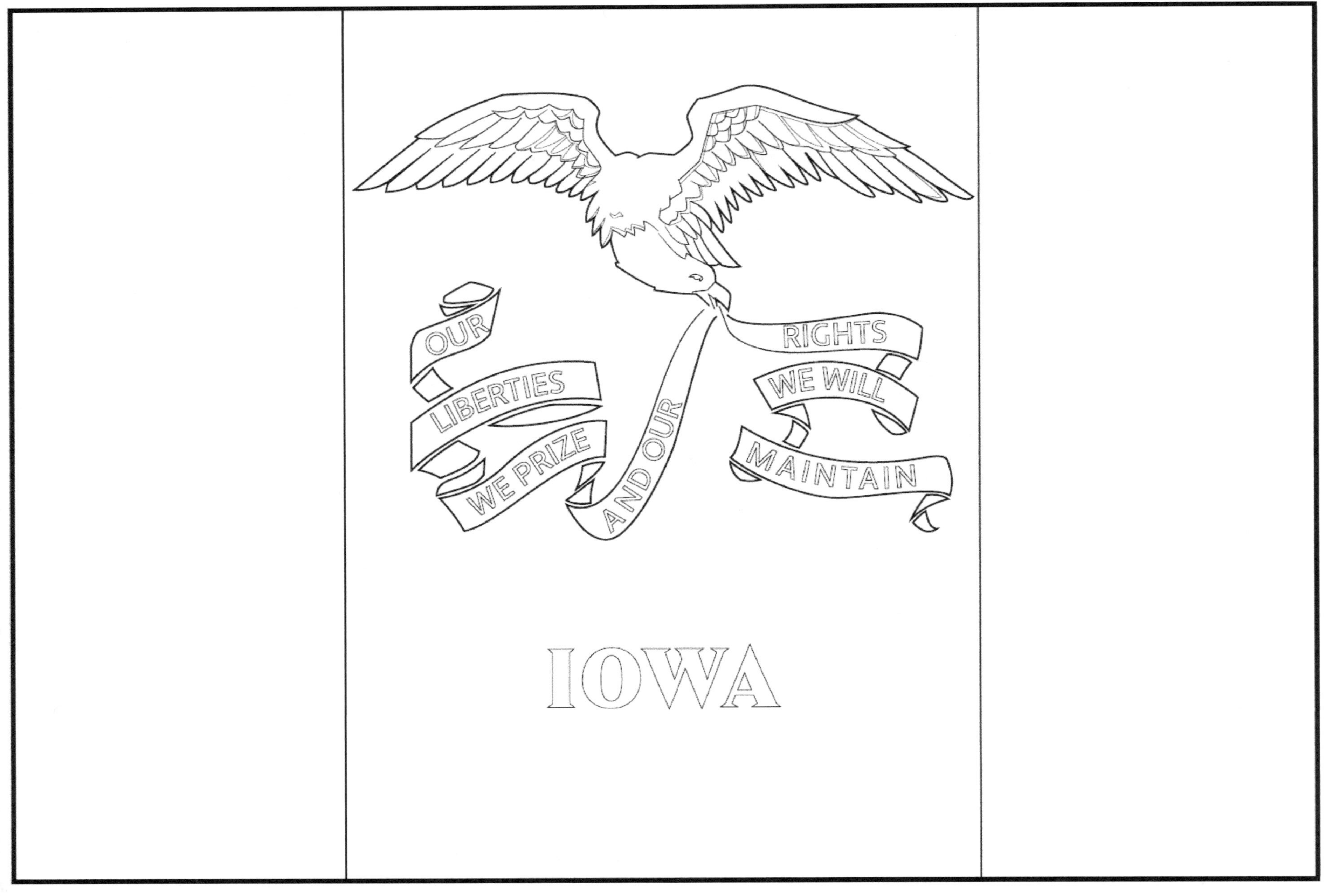

IOWA

AD ASTRA PER ASPERA

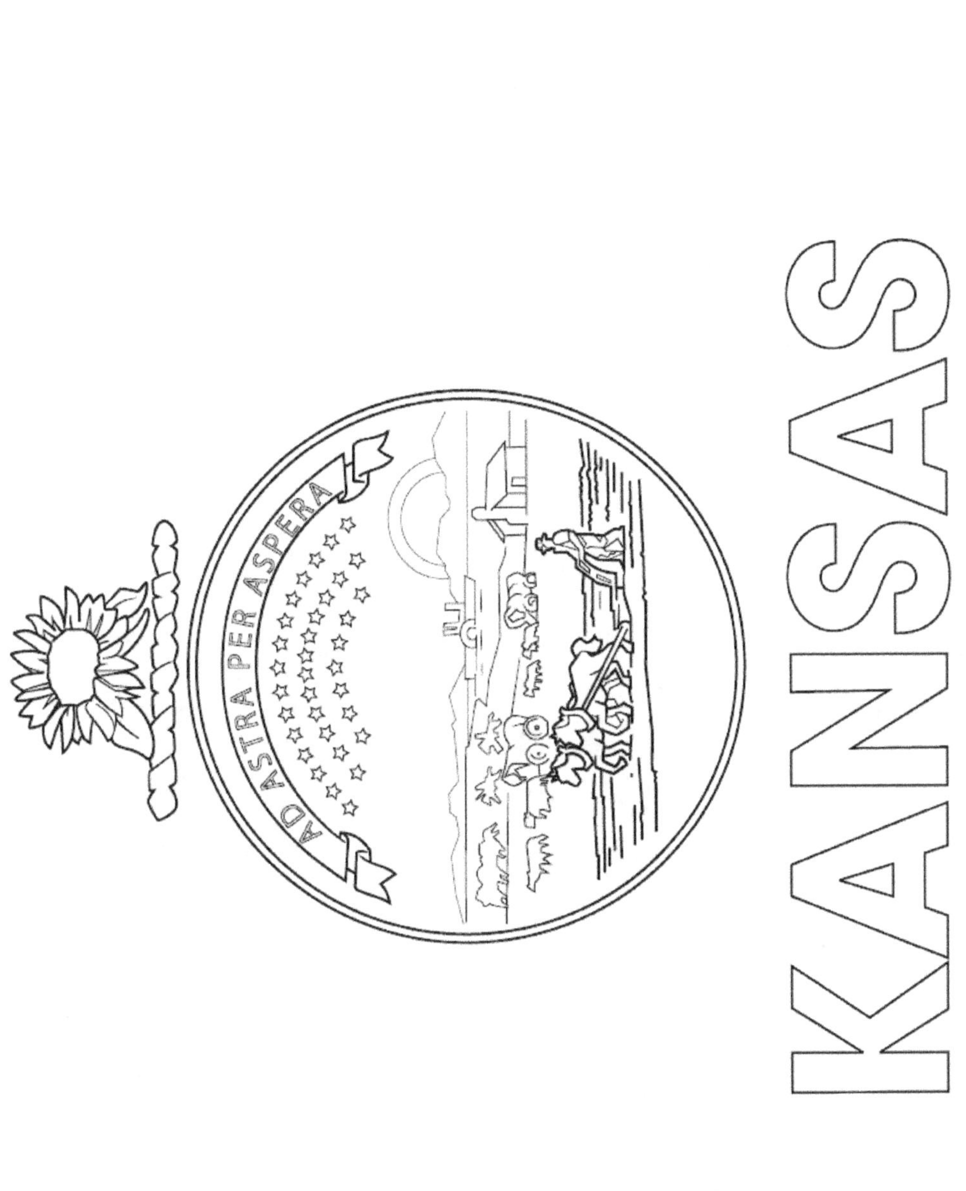

KANSAS

COMMONWEALTH OF KENTUCKY
UNITED WE STAND
DIVIDED WE FALL

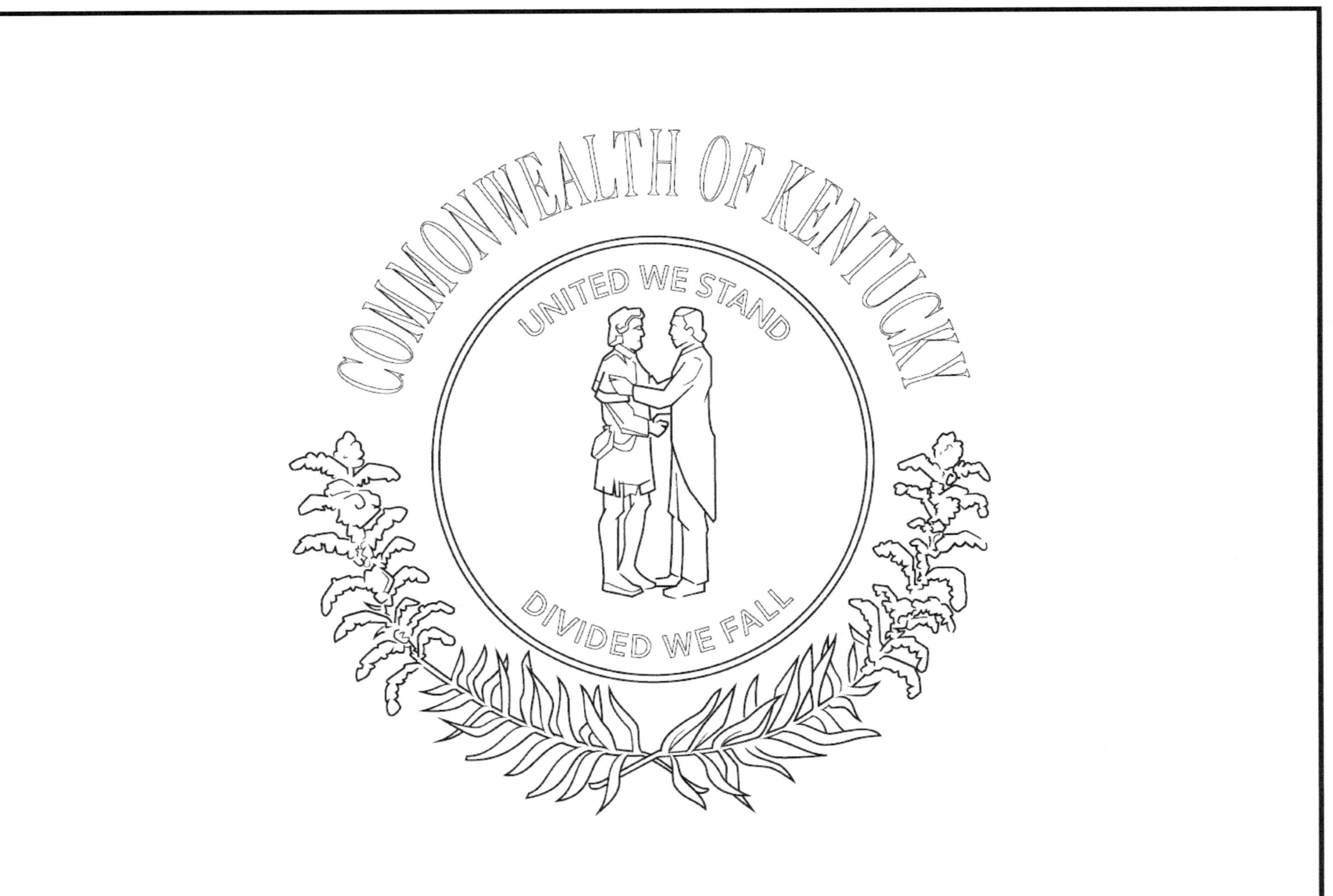

KENTUCKY

UNION JUSTICE CONFIDENCE

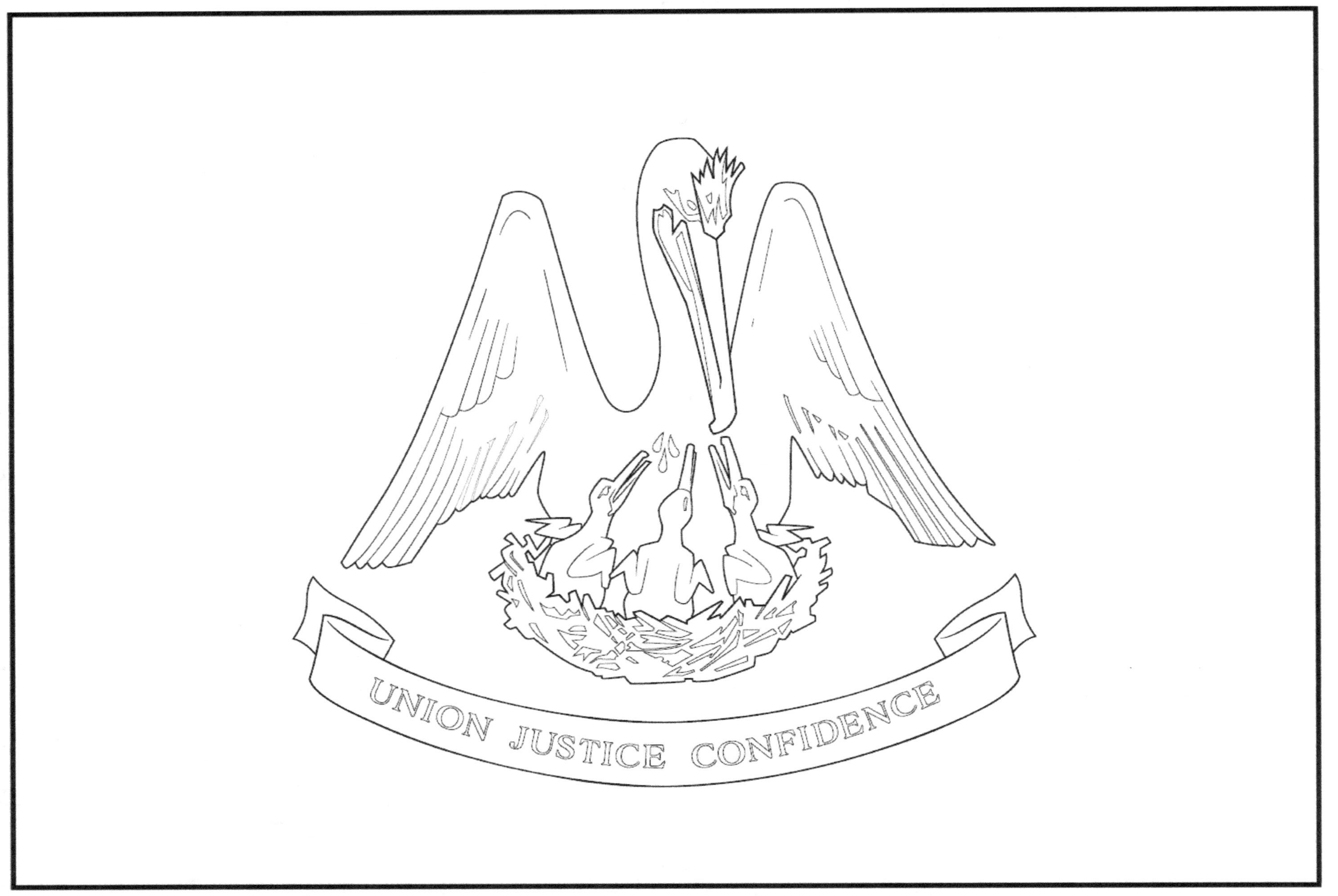

LOUISIANA

DIRIGO
MAINE

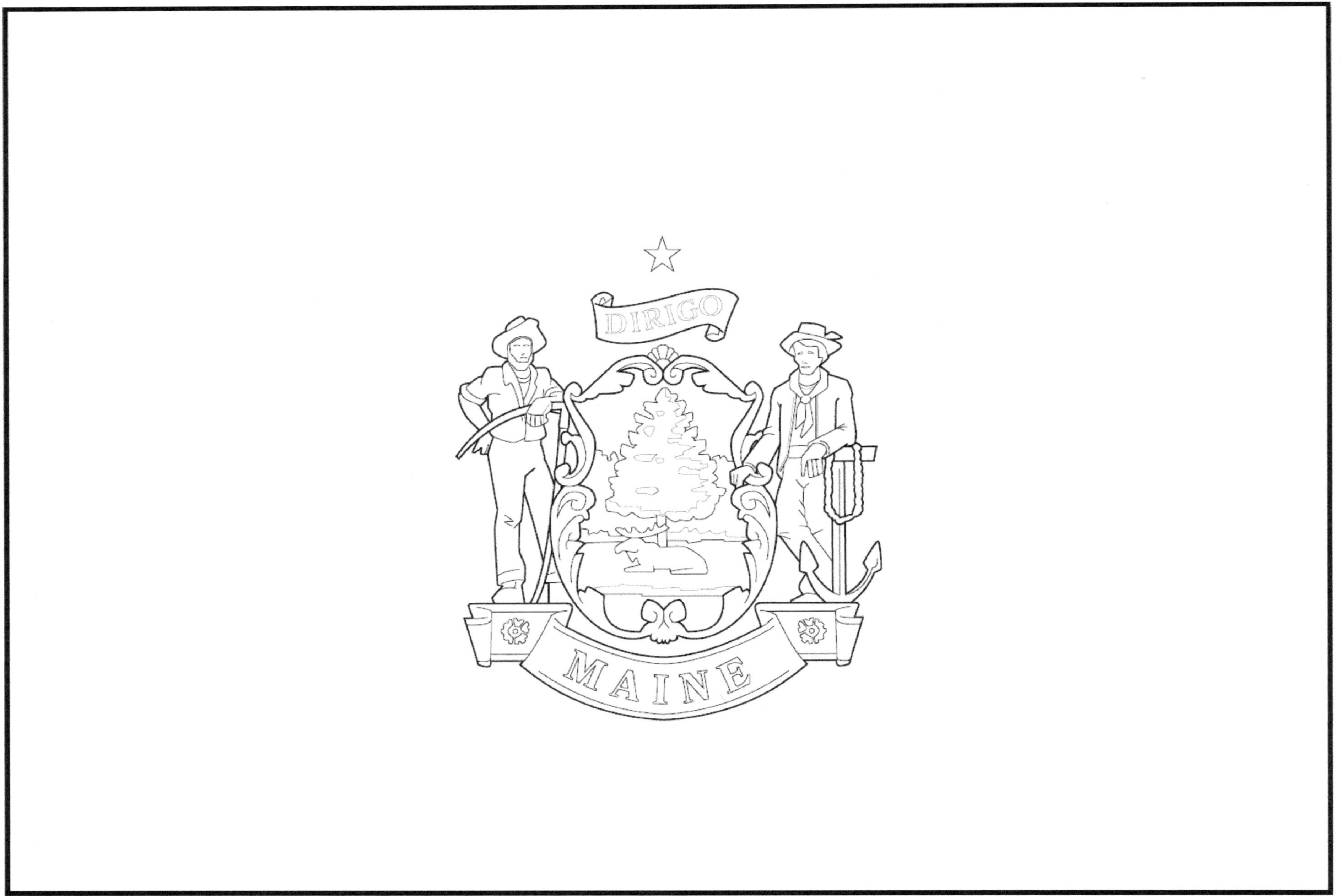

MAINE

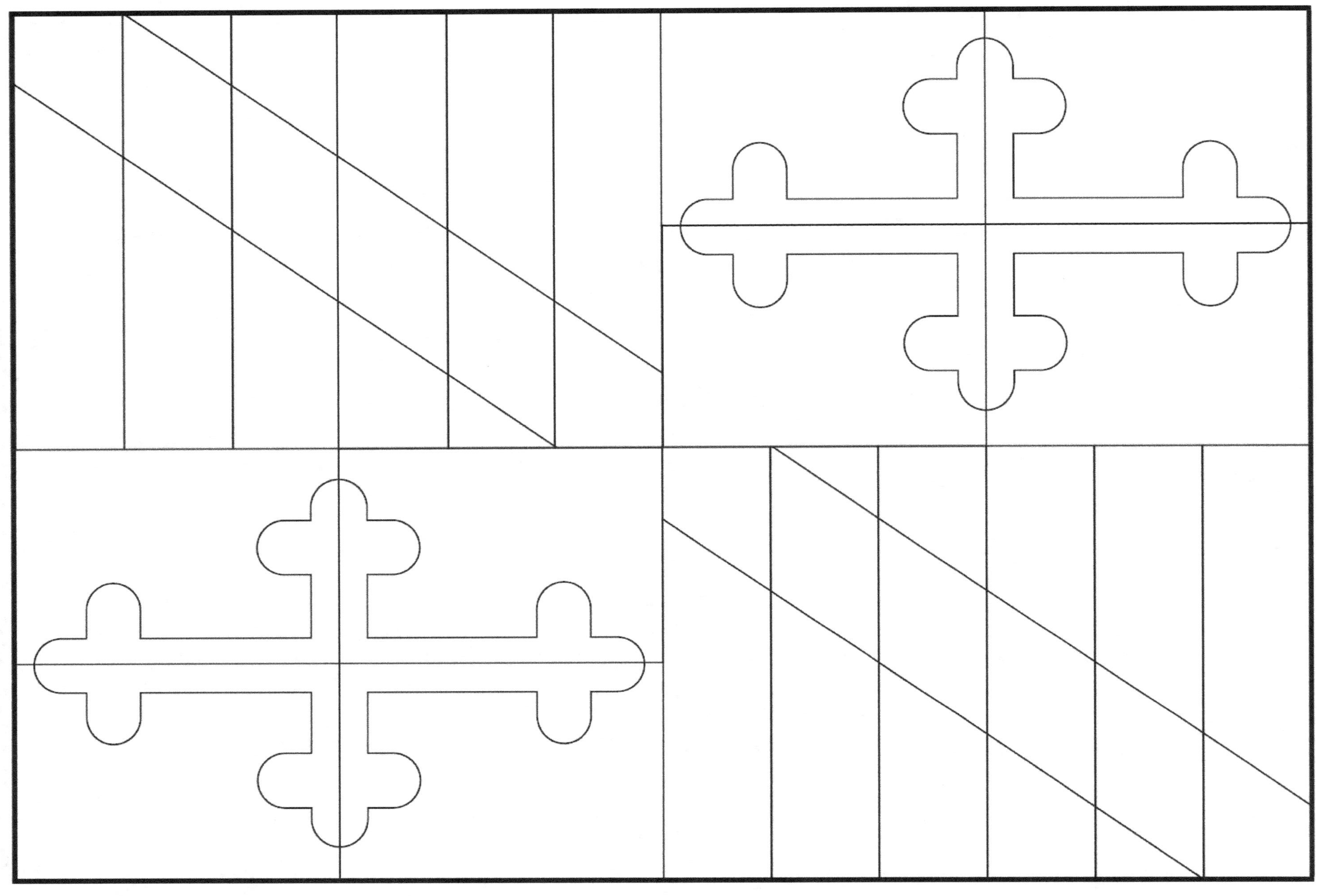

MARYLAND

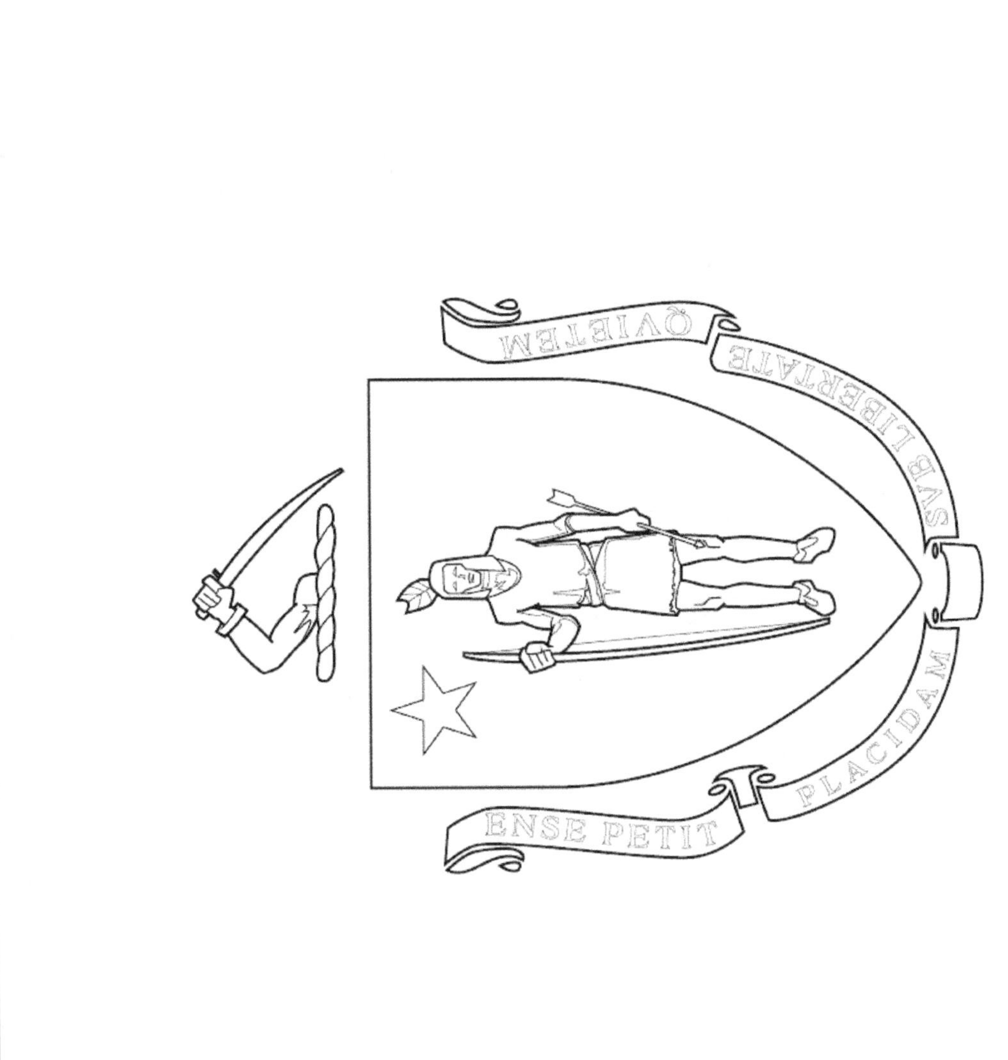

MASSACHUSETTS

E PLURIBUS UNUM
TUEBOR
SI QUÆRIS PENINSULAM AMŒNAM
CIRCUMSPICE

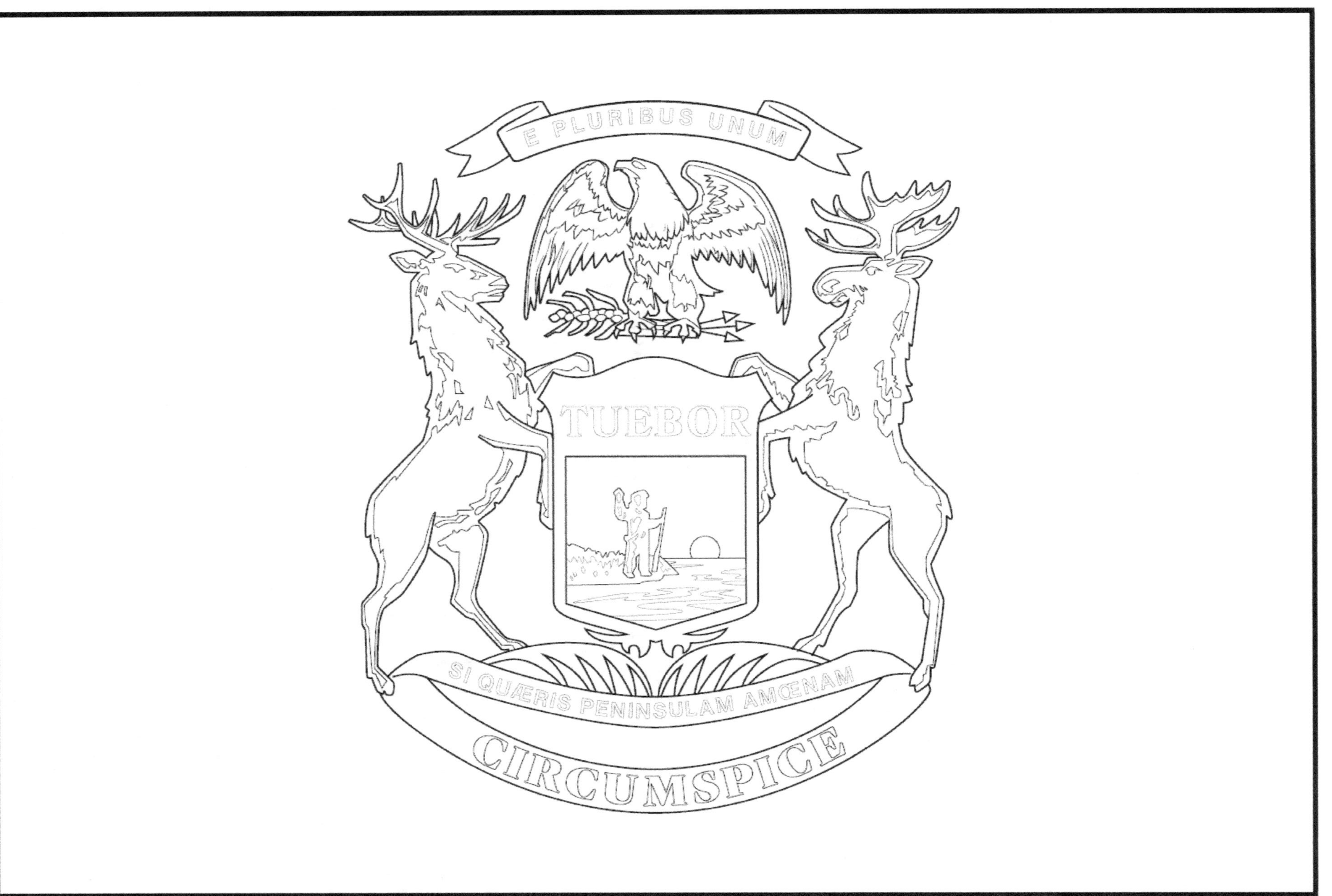

MICHIGAN

1858
L'ETOILE DU NORD
1819
1893
MINNESOTA

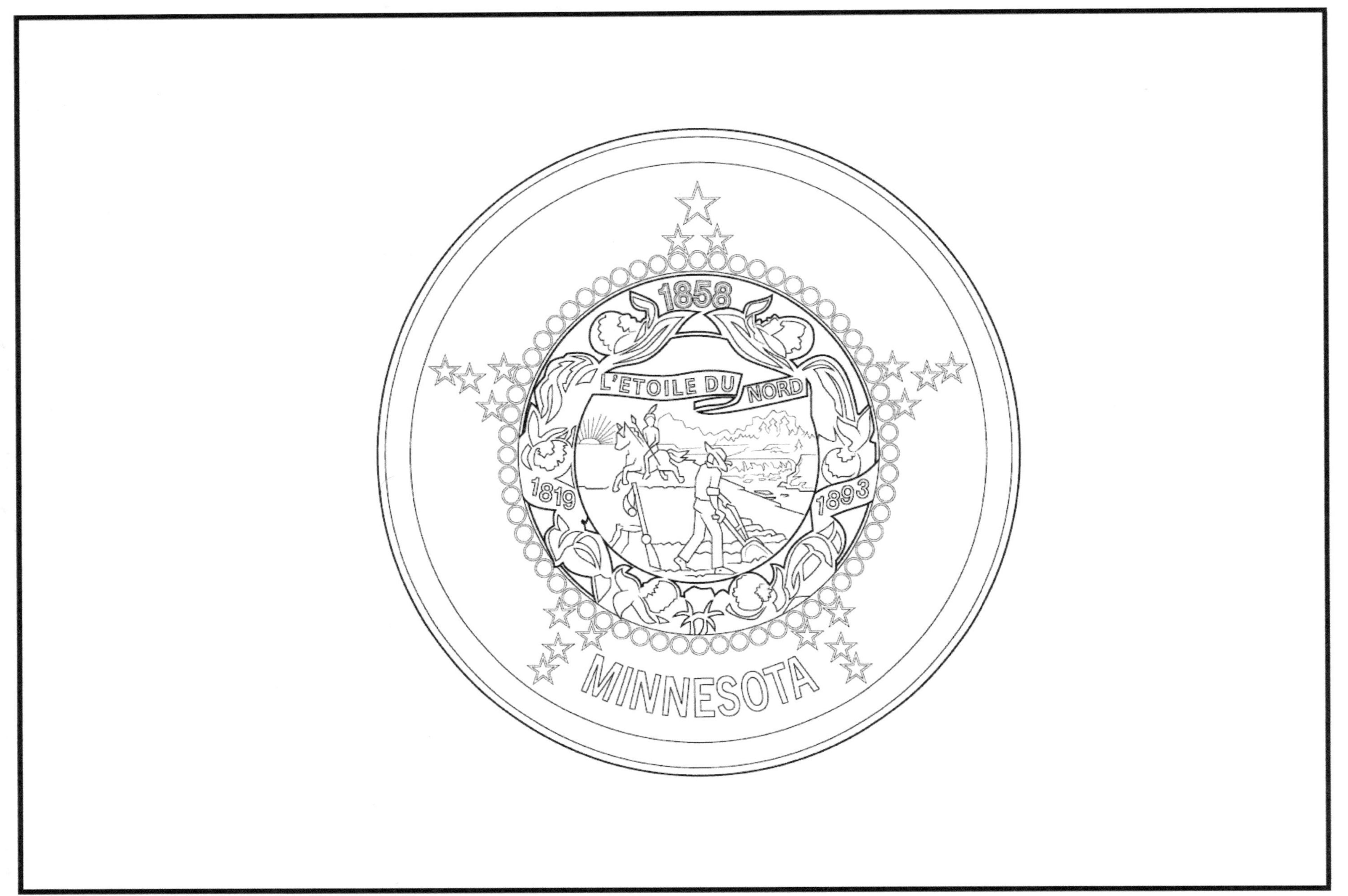

MINNESOTA

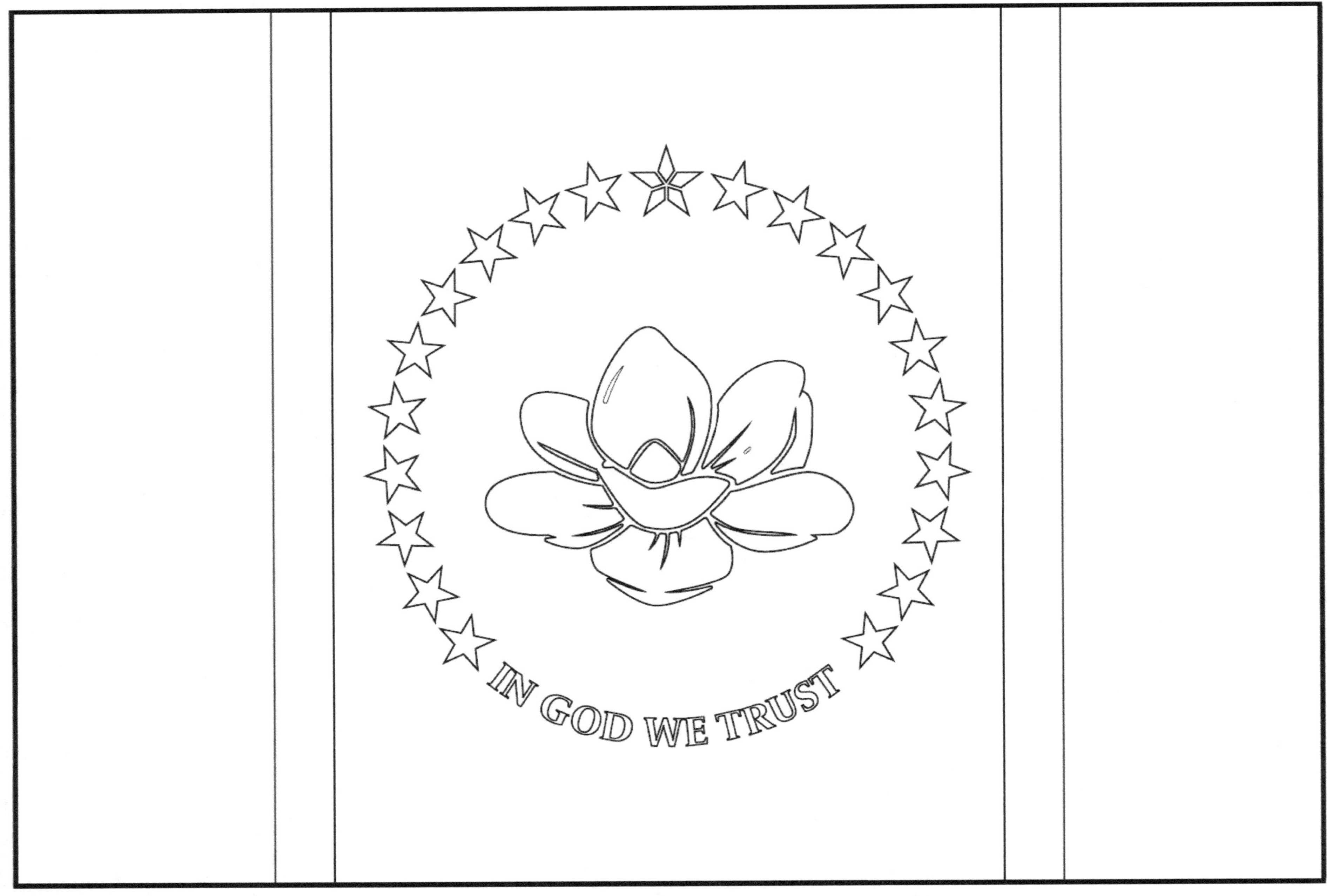

MISSISSIPPI

UNITED WE STAND
DIVIDED WE FALL
SALIS
LEX ESTO
OPULI SUPREMA
MDCCCXX

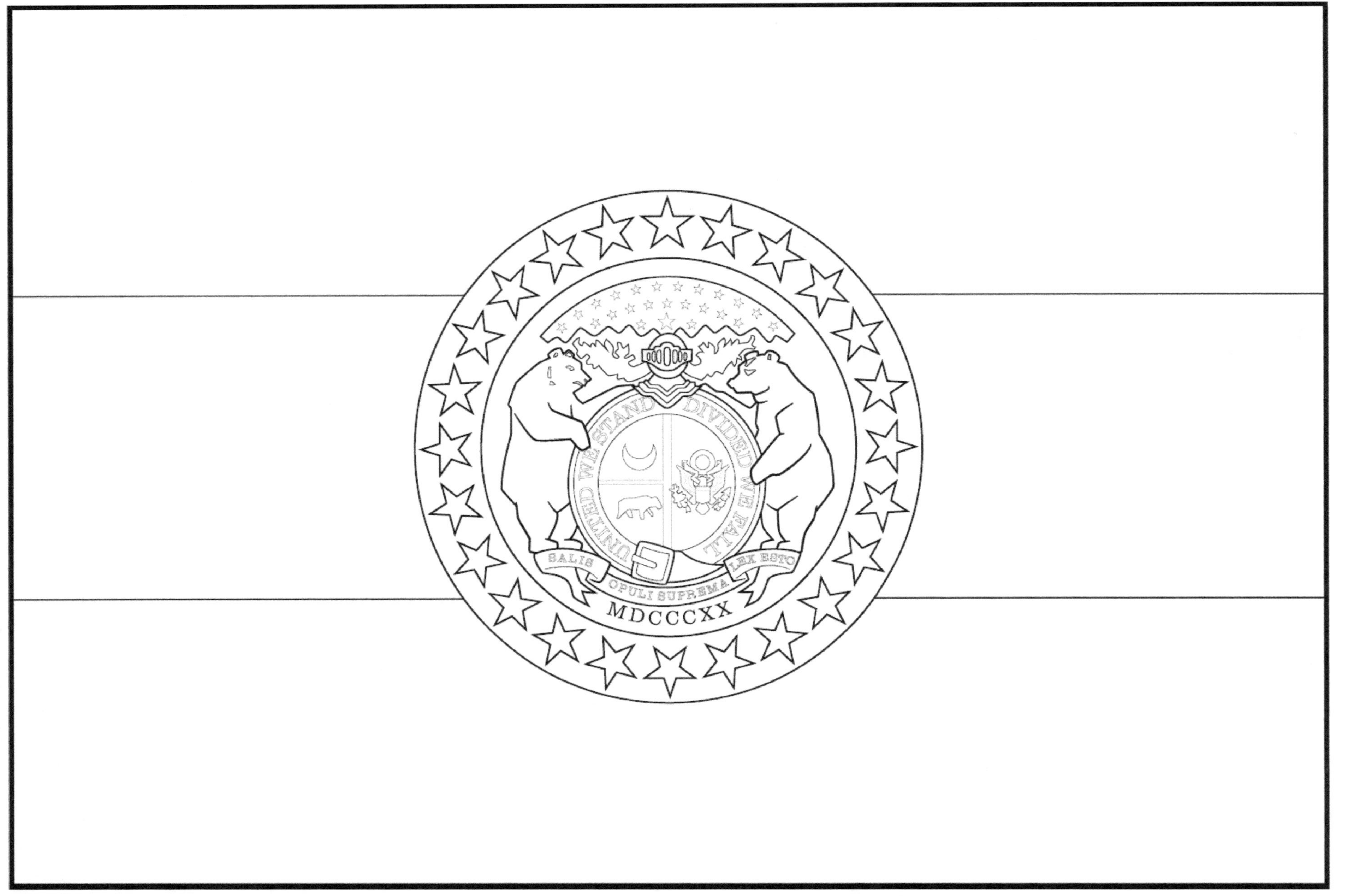

MISSOURI

THE GREAT SEAL OF THE STATE OF MONTANA
ORO -Y- PLATA

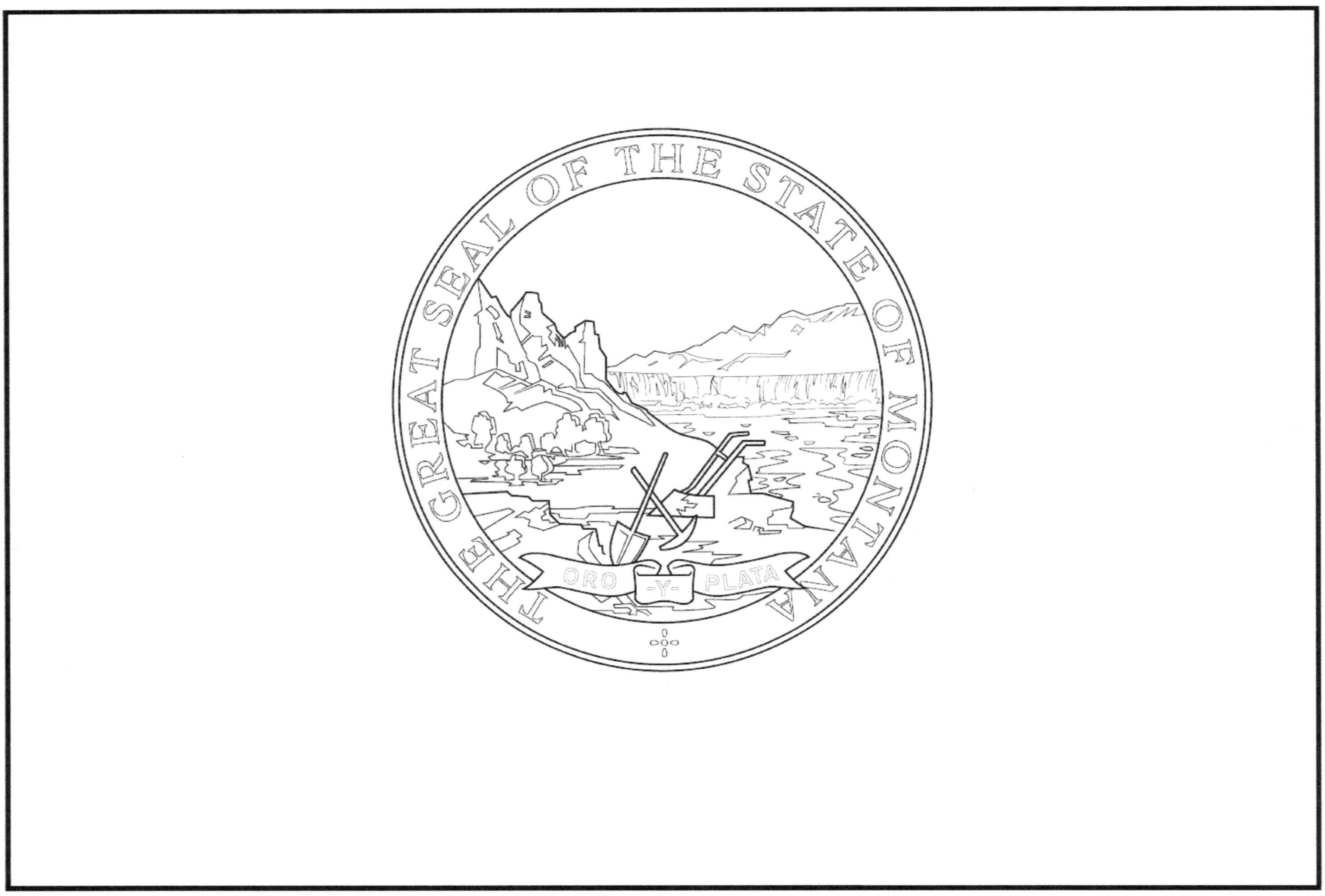

MONTANA

GREAT SEAL OF THE STATE OF NEBRASKA
BEFORE
EQUALITY
THE LAW
MARCH 1ST 1867

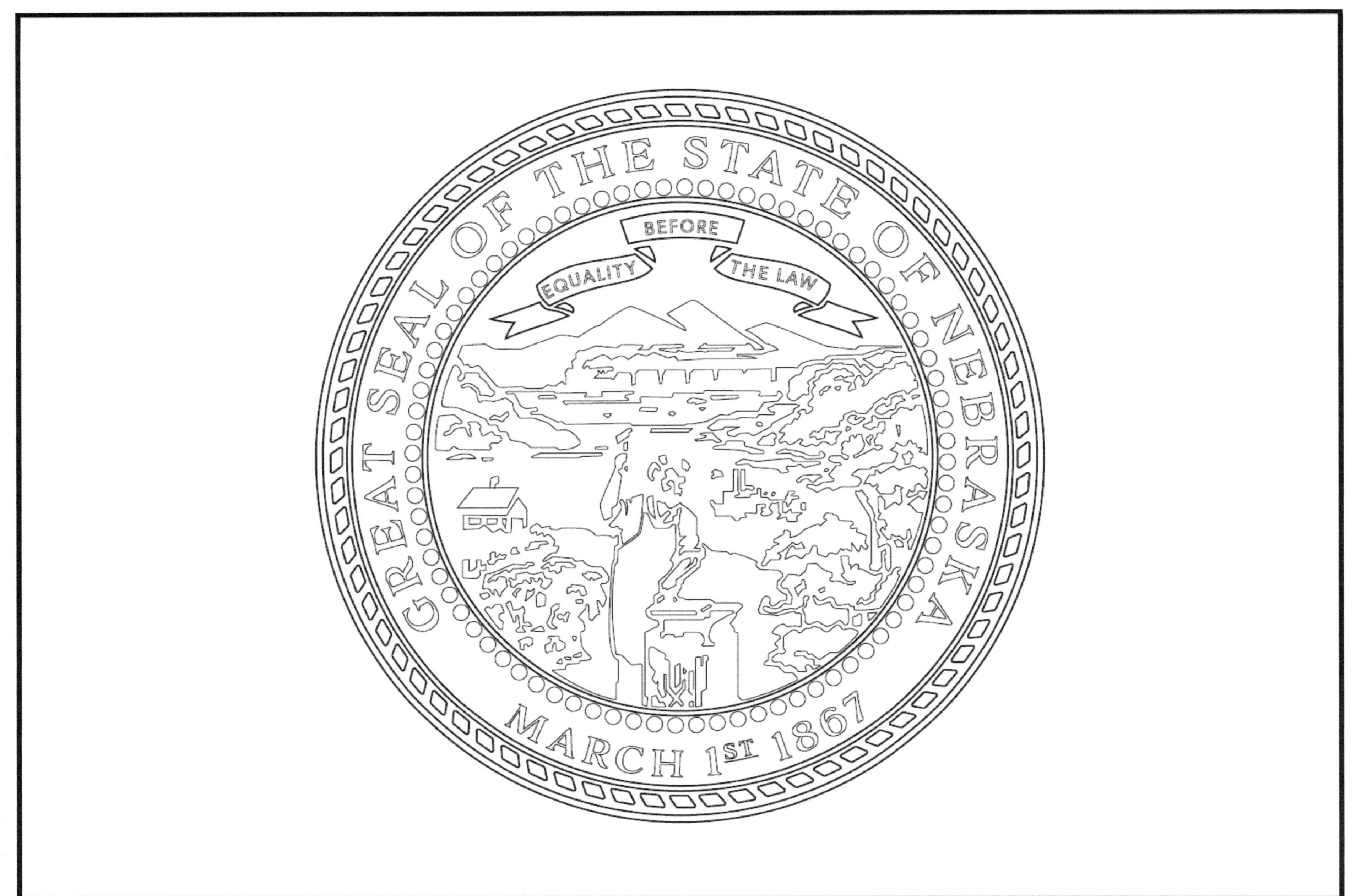

NEBRASKA

BATTLE BORN
NEVADA

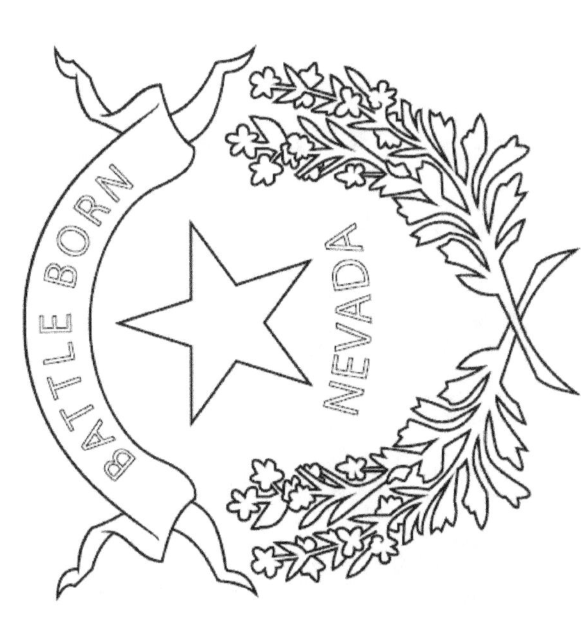

NEVADA

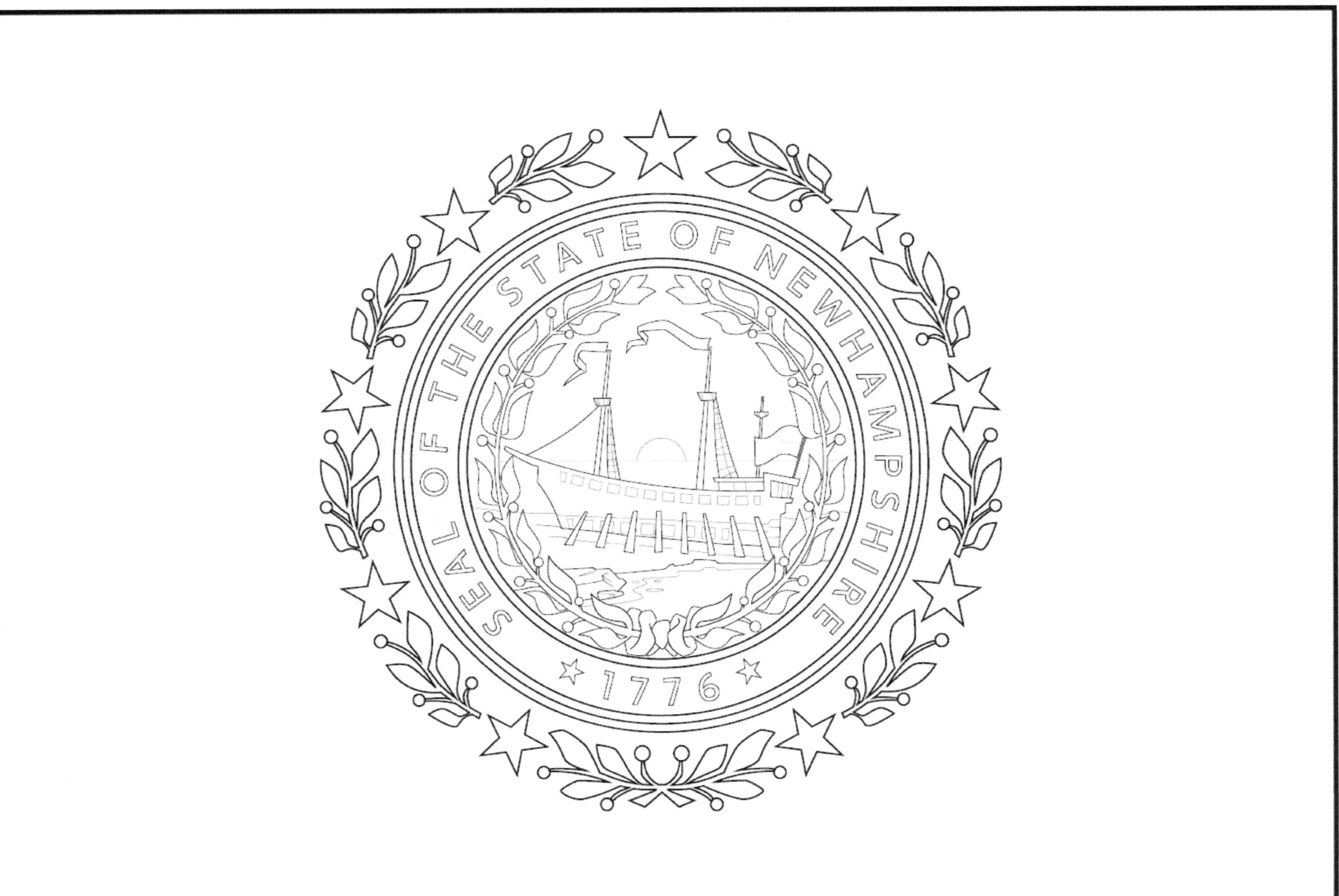

NEW HAMPSHIRE

LIBERTY AND PROSPERITY
1776

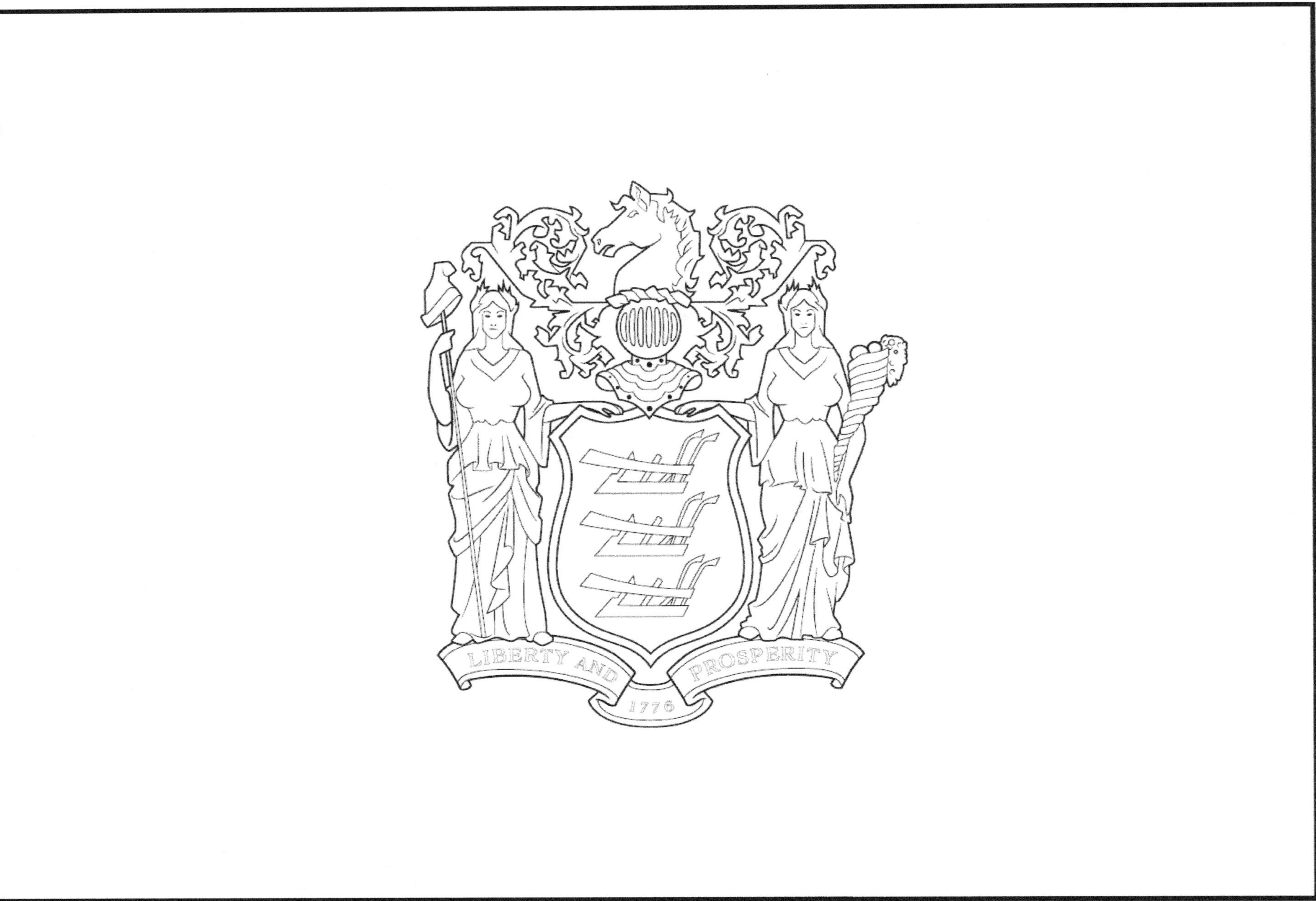

NEW JERSEY

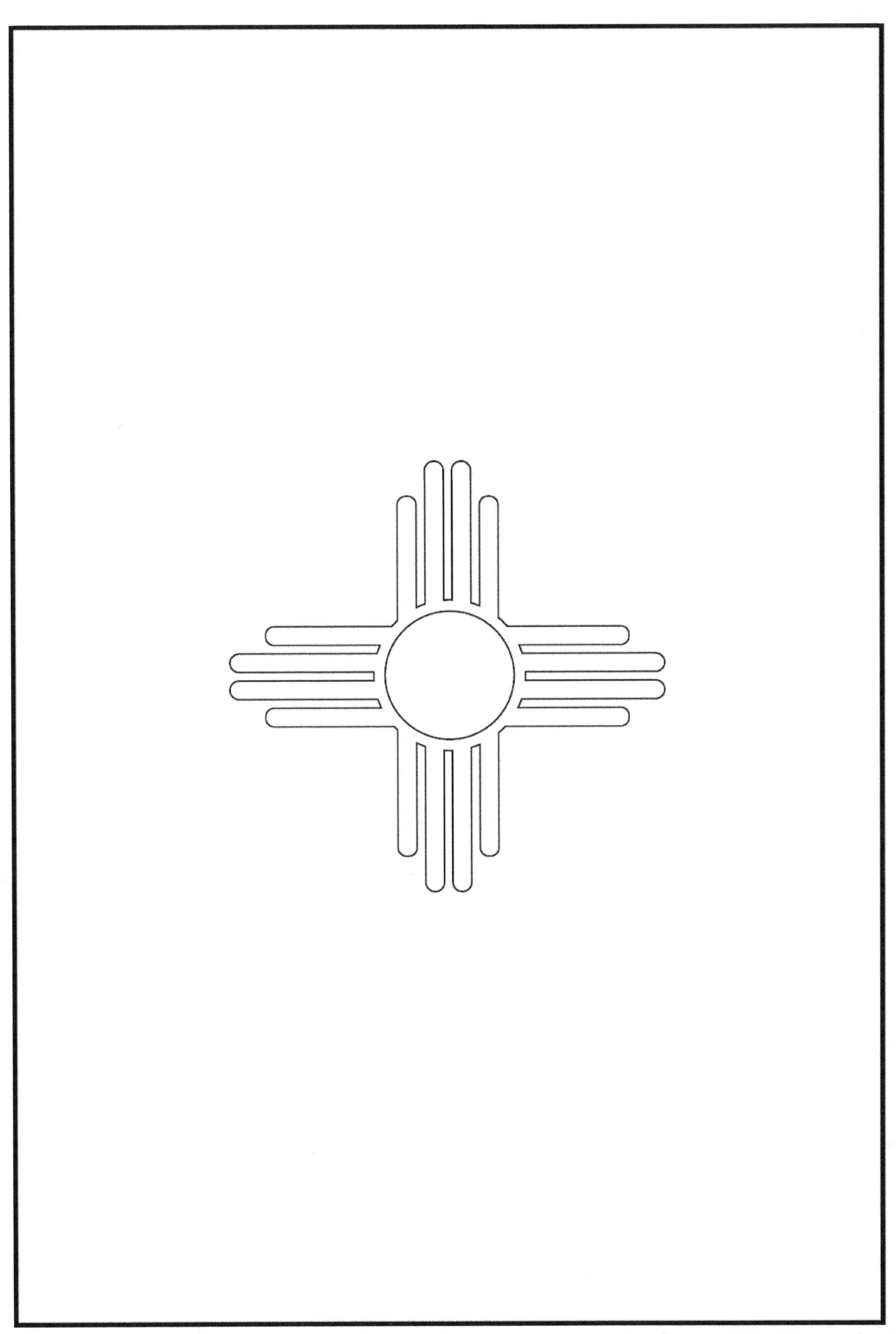

NEW MEXICO

EXCELSIOR
E PLURIBUS UNUM

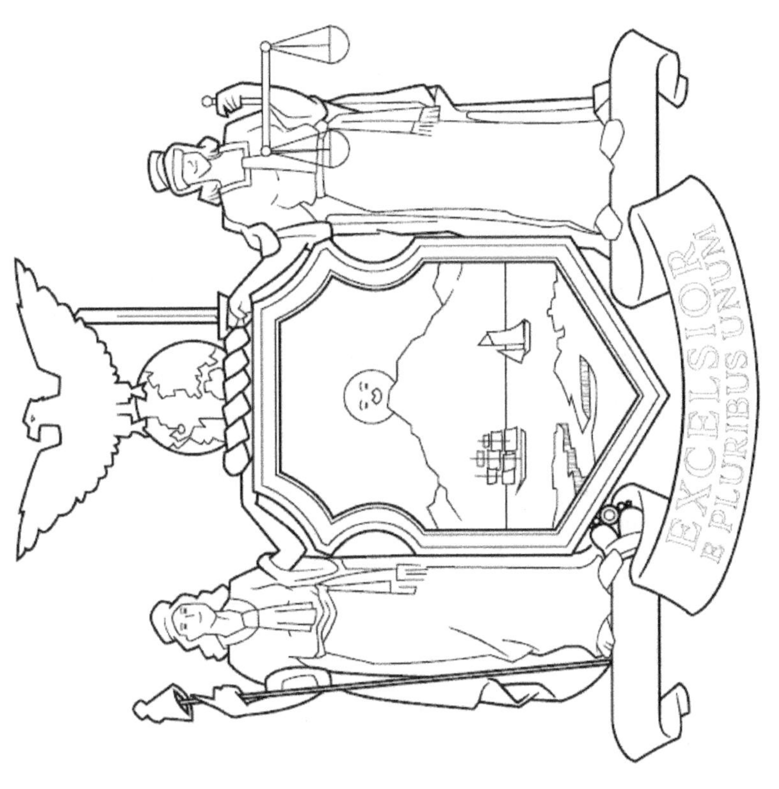

NEW YORK

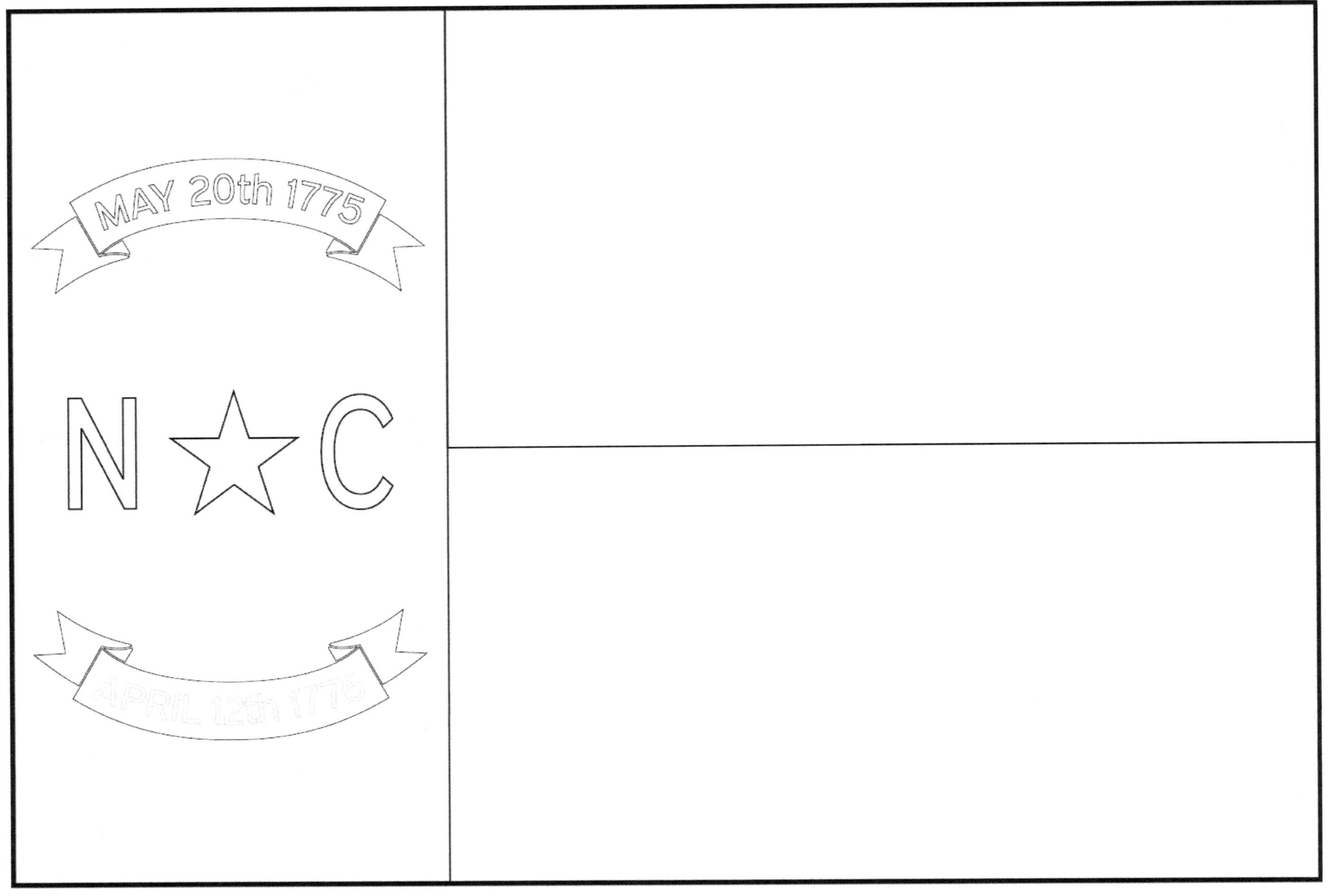

NORTH CAROLINA

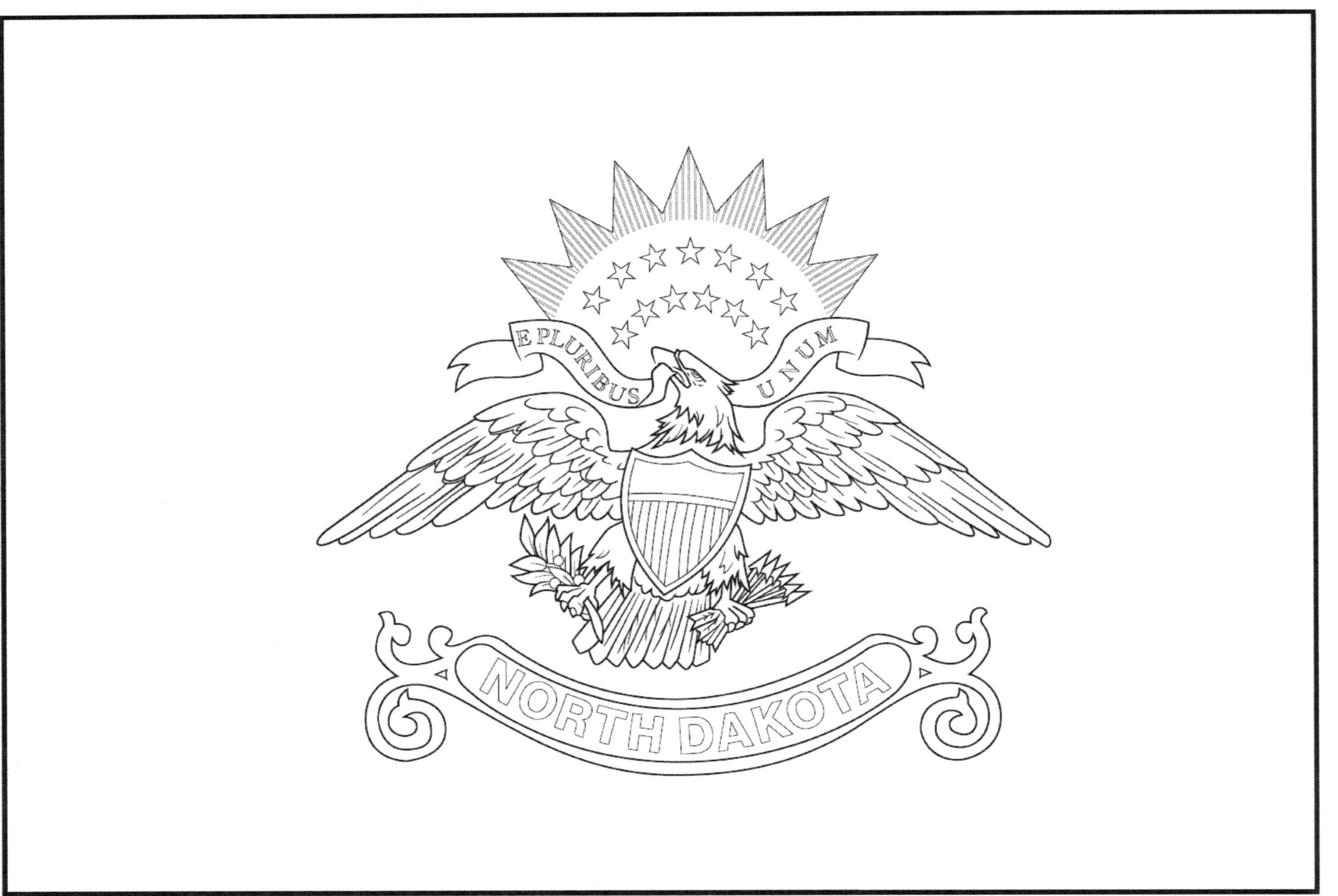

NORTH DAKOTA

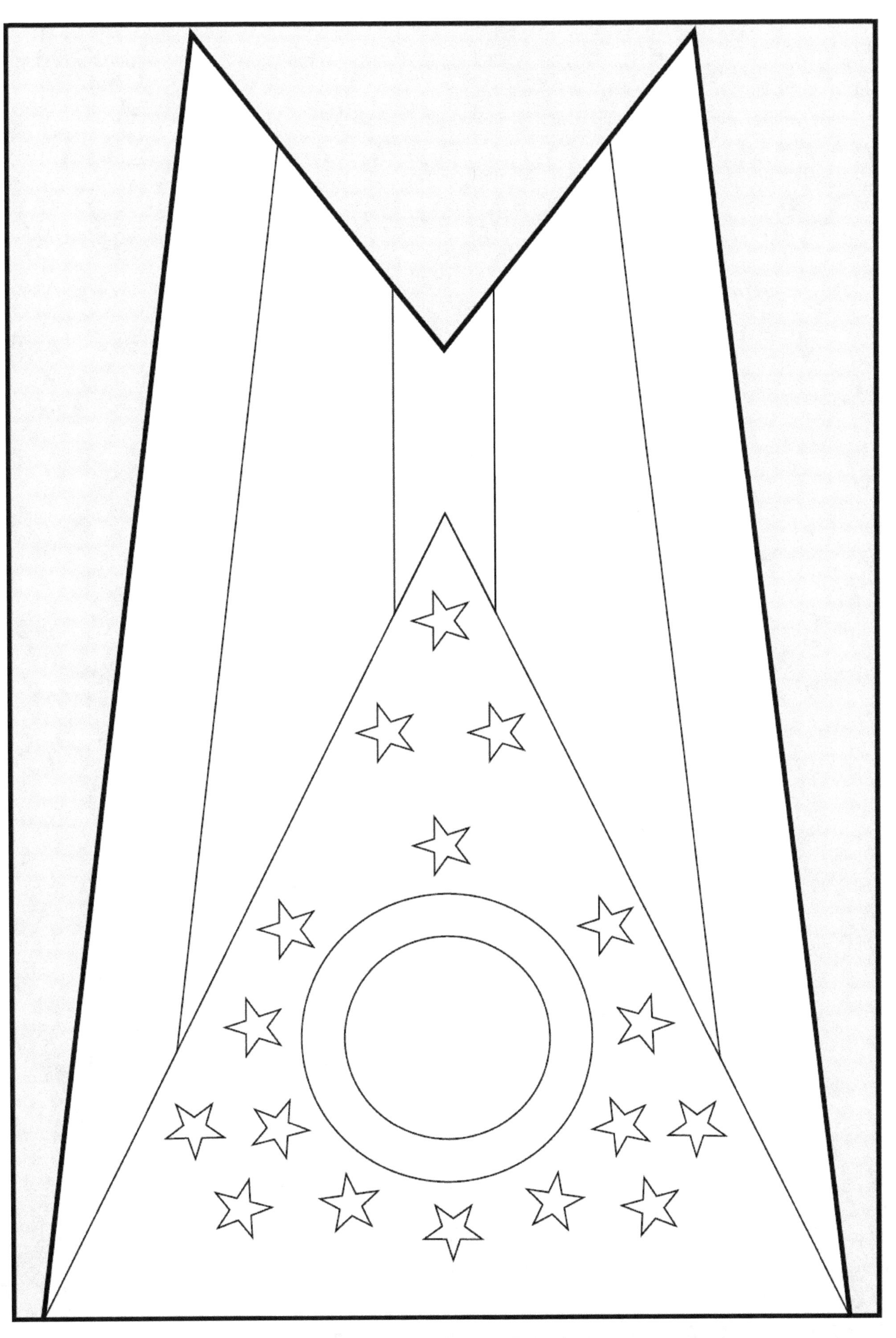

OHIO

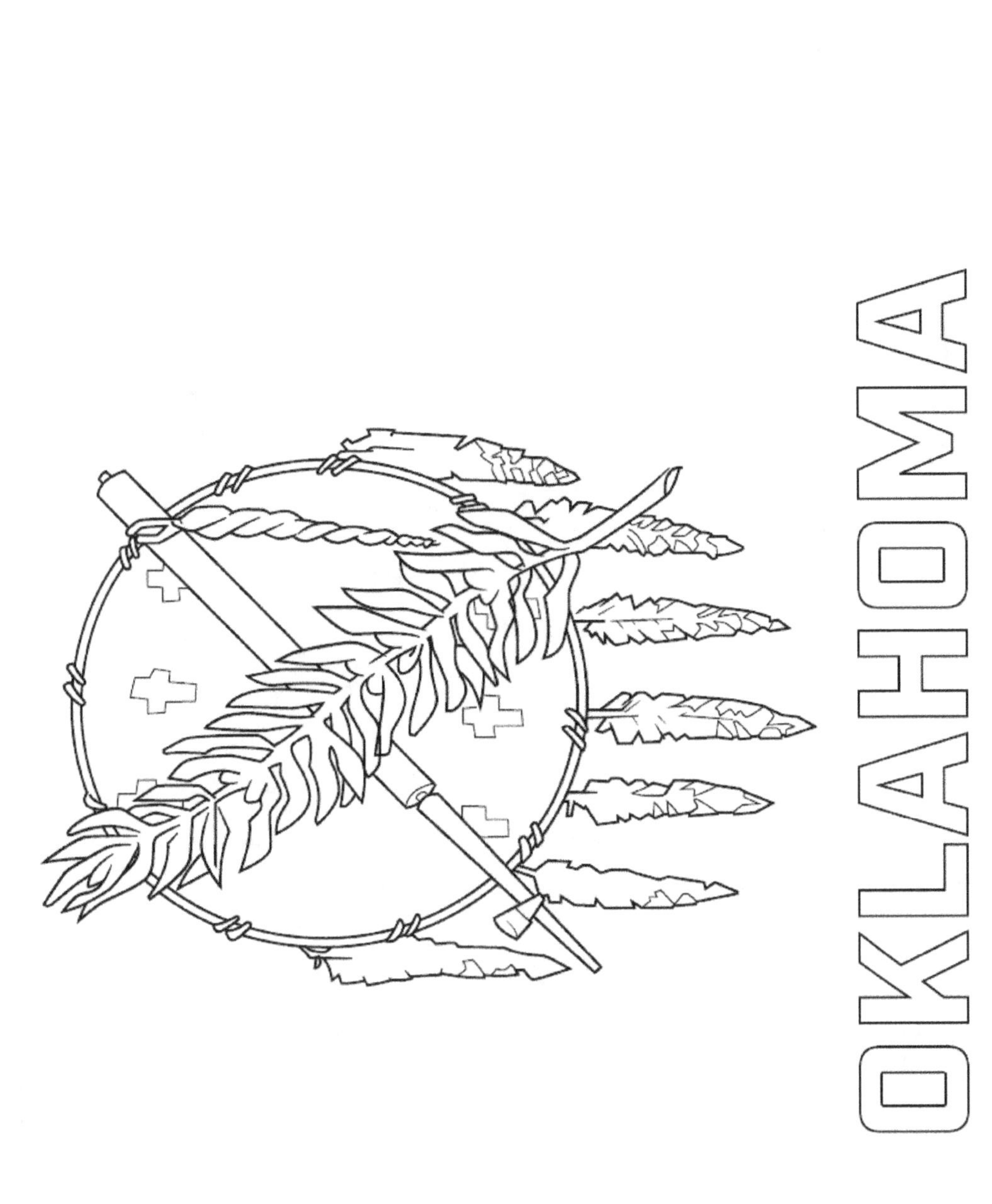

OKLAHOMA

STATE OF OF OREGON
THE UNION
1859

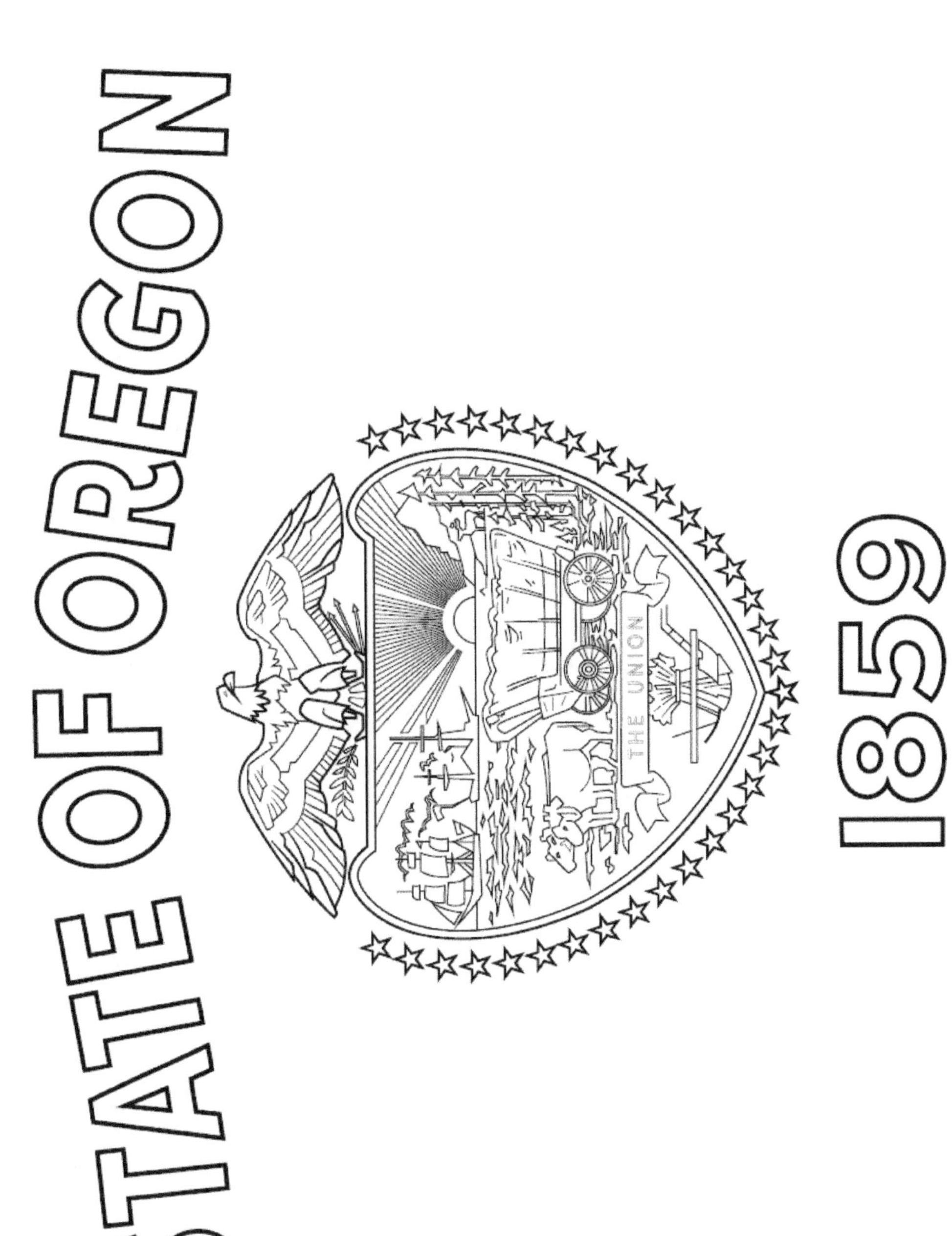

OREGON

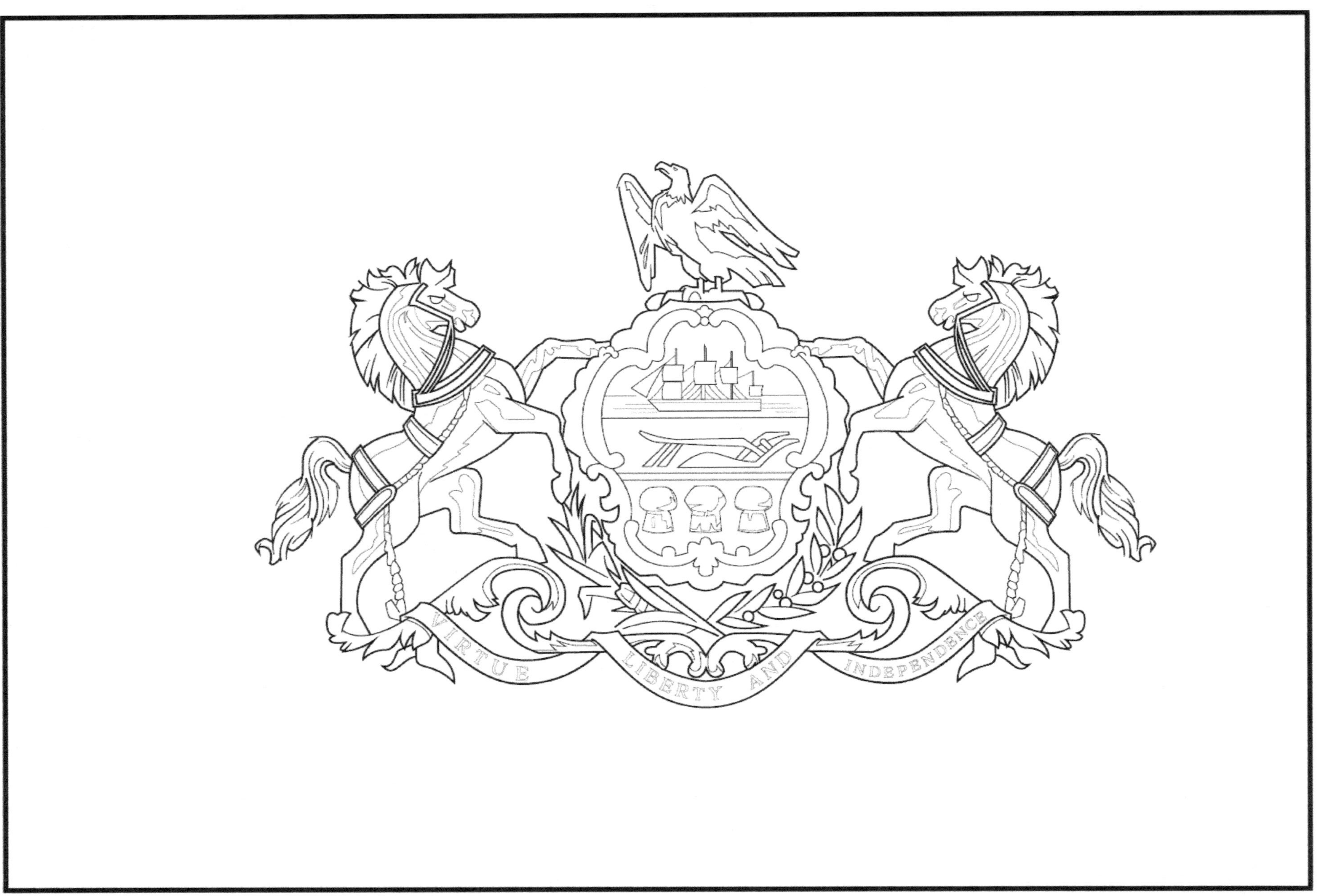

PENNSYLVANIA

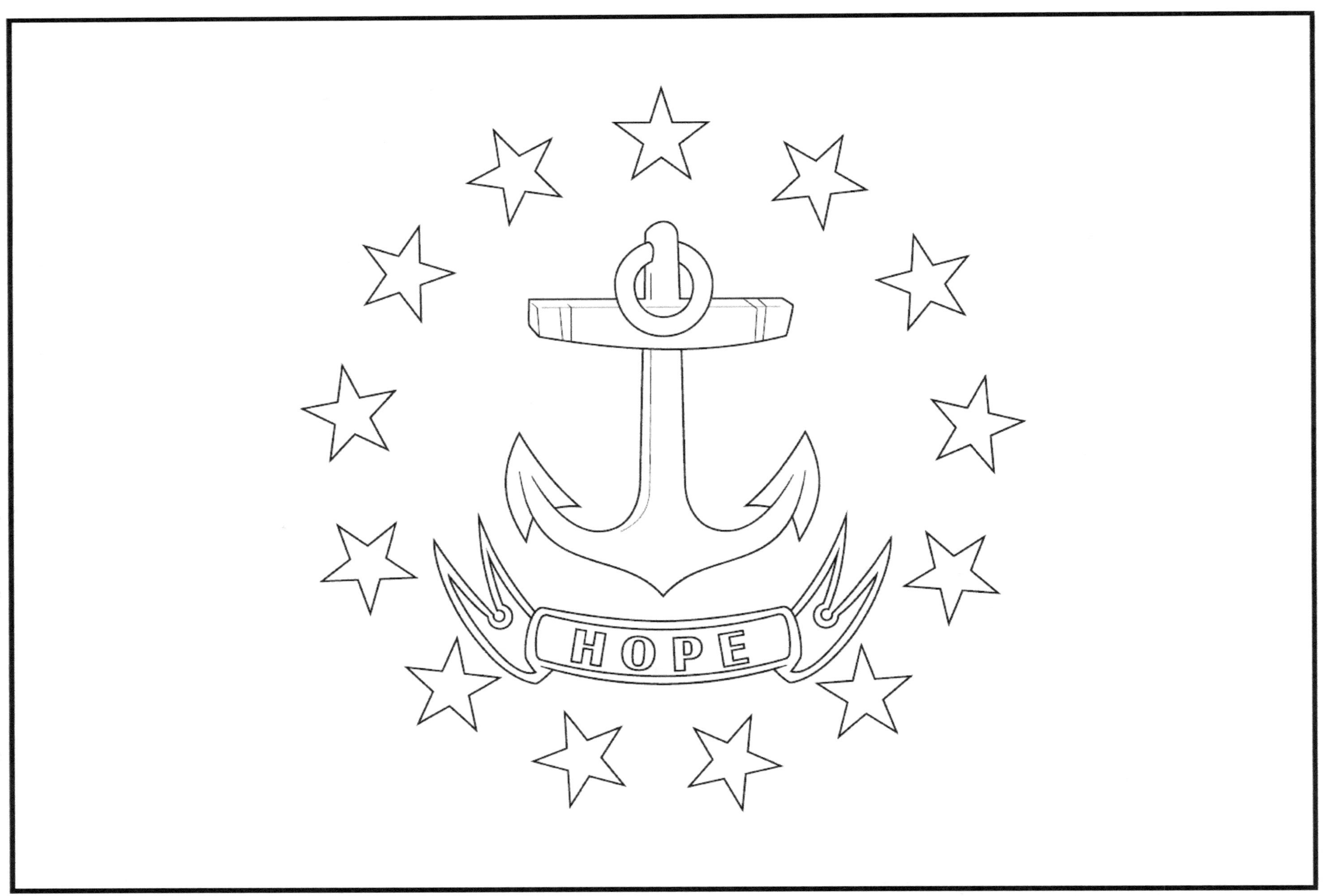

RHODE ISLAND

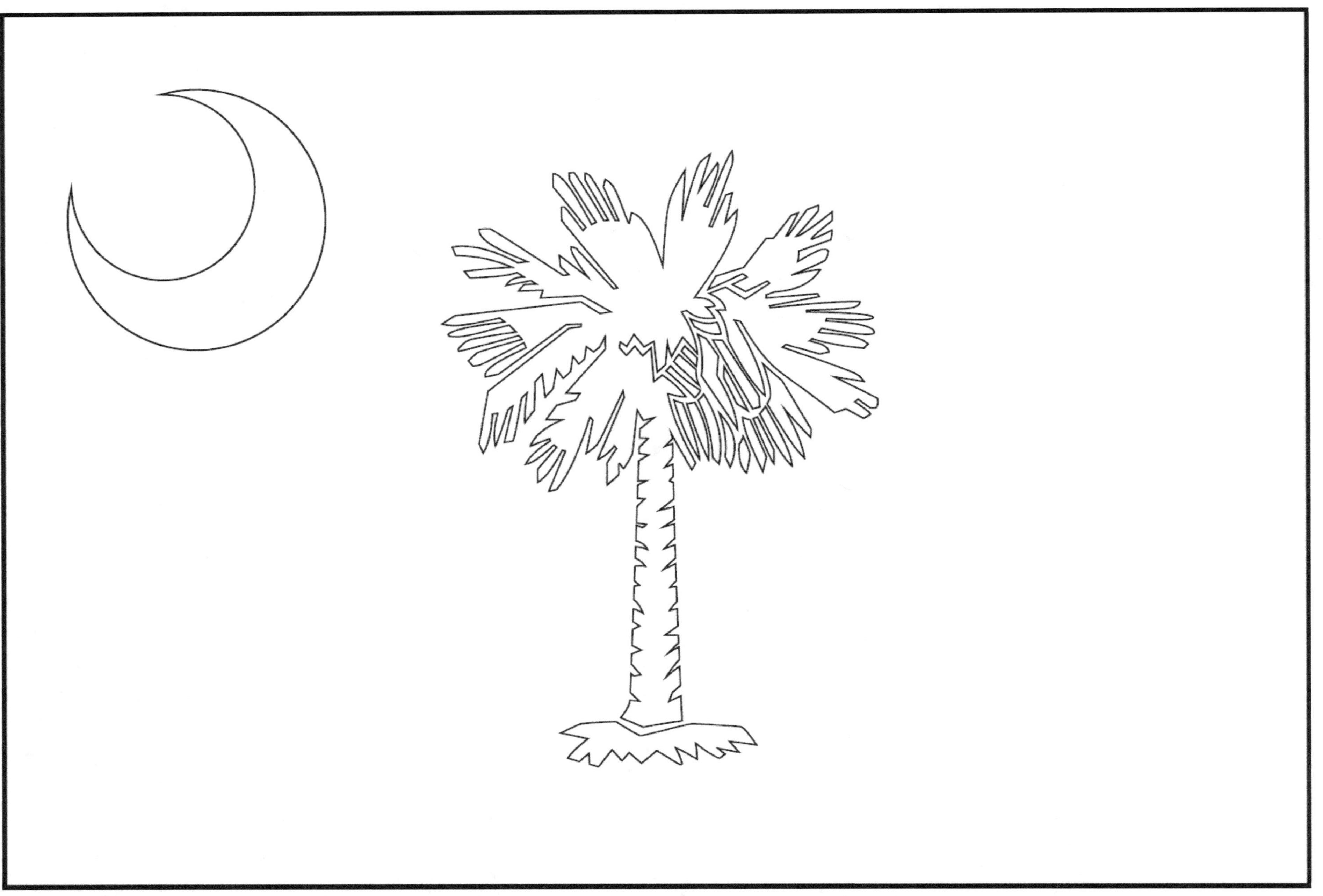

SOUTH CAROLINA

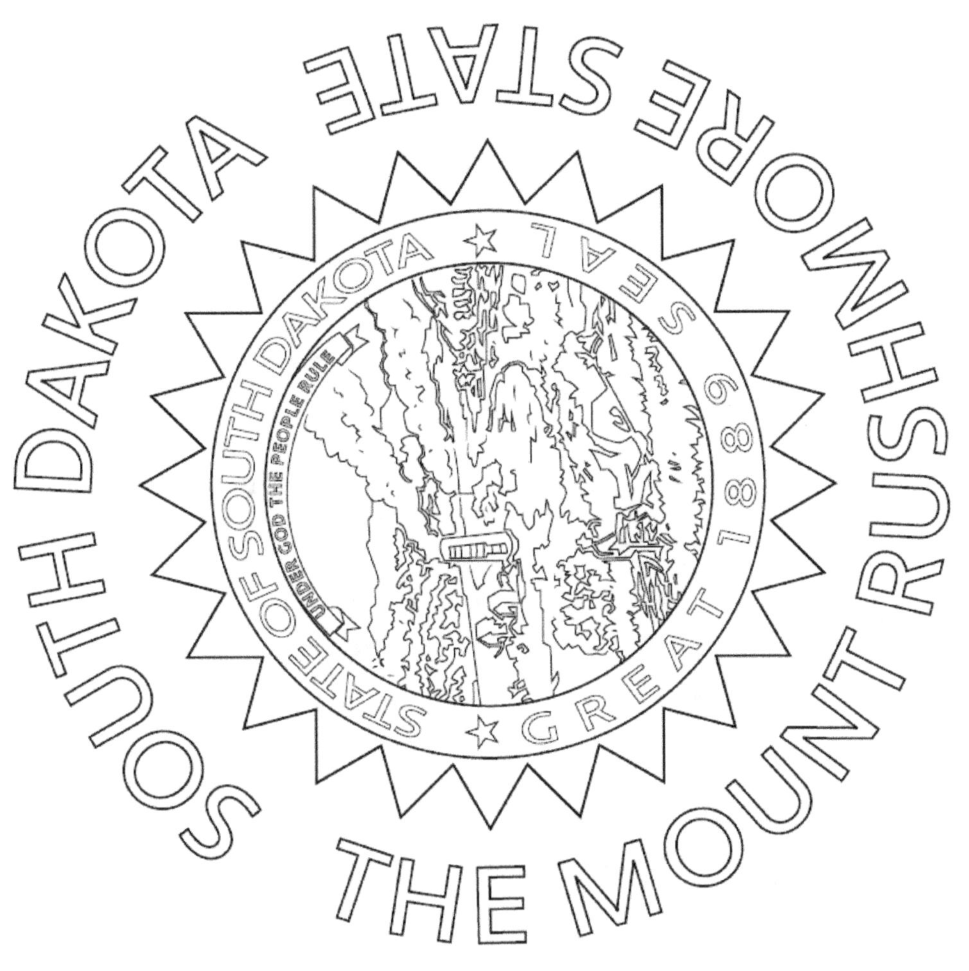

SOUTH DAKOTA

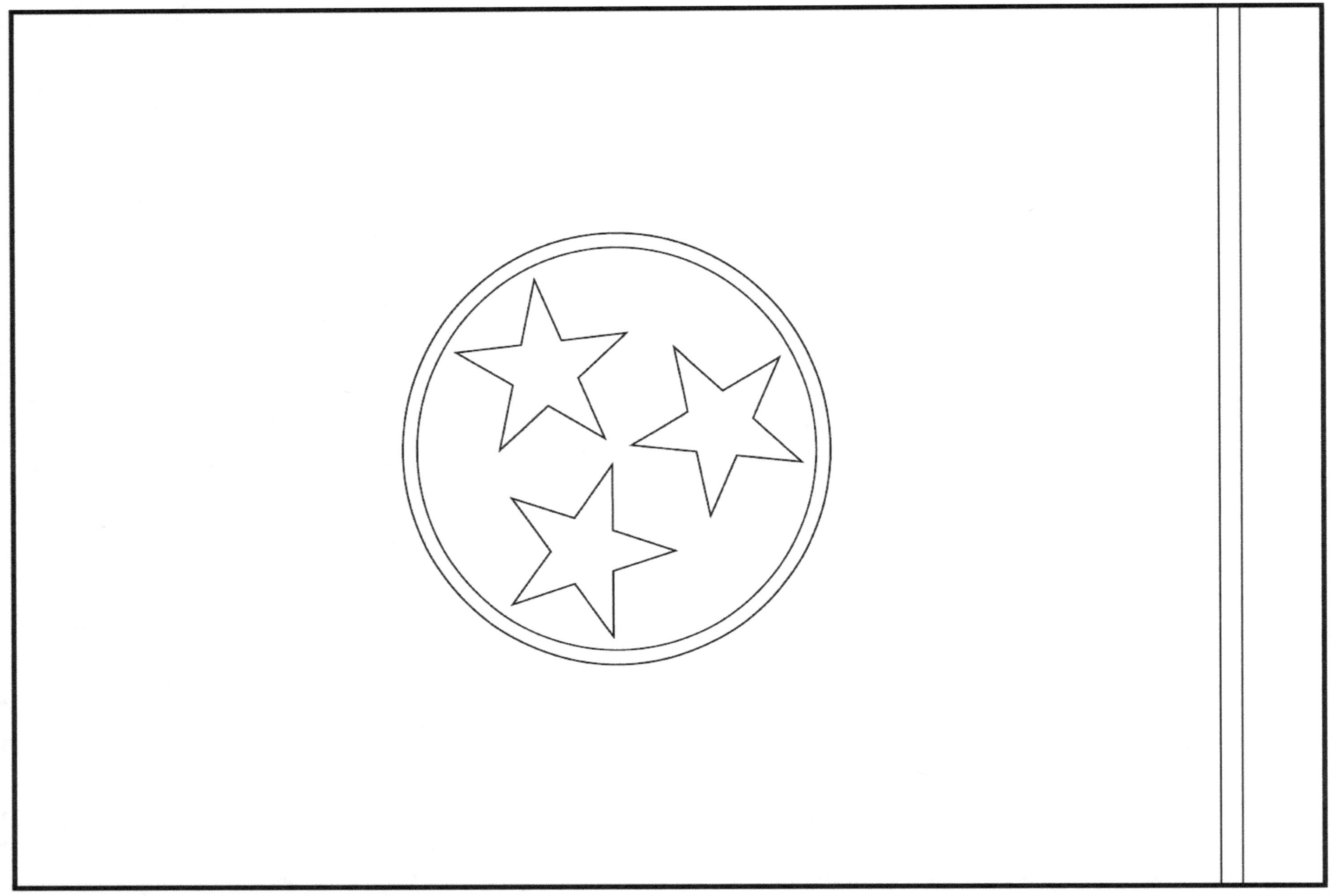

TENNESSEE

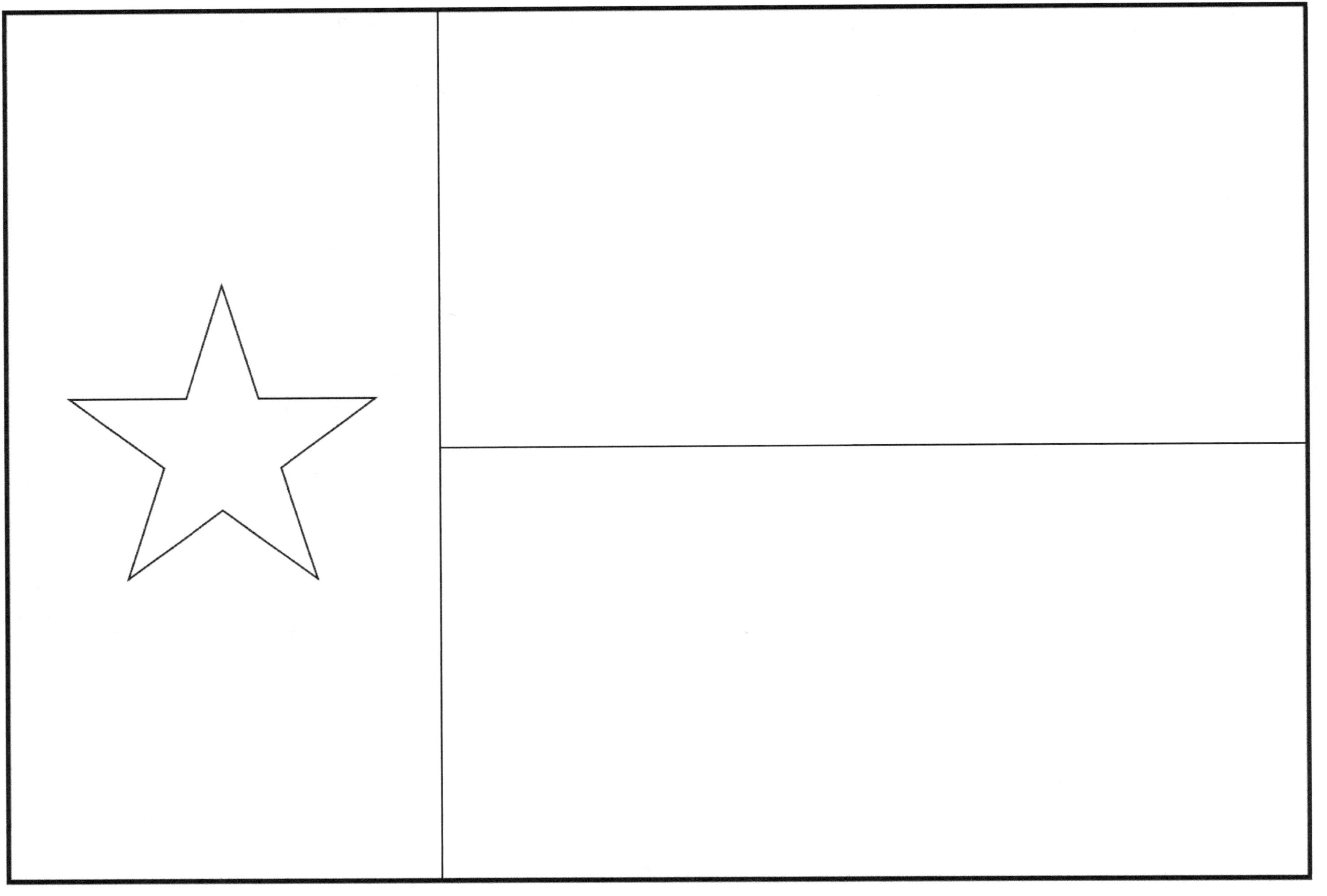

TEXAS

INDUSTRY
UTAH
1847
1896

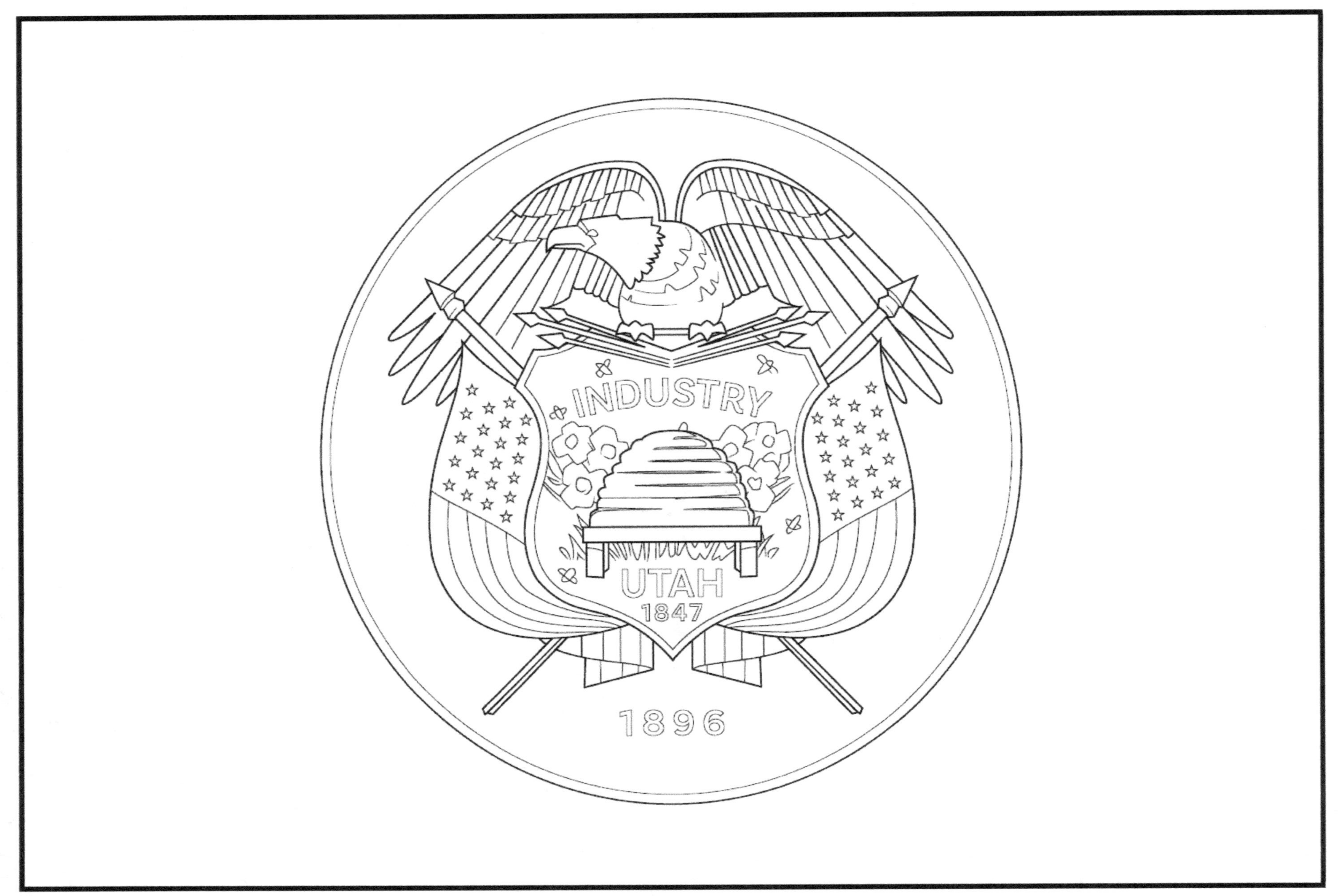

UTAH

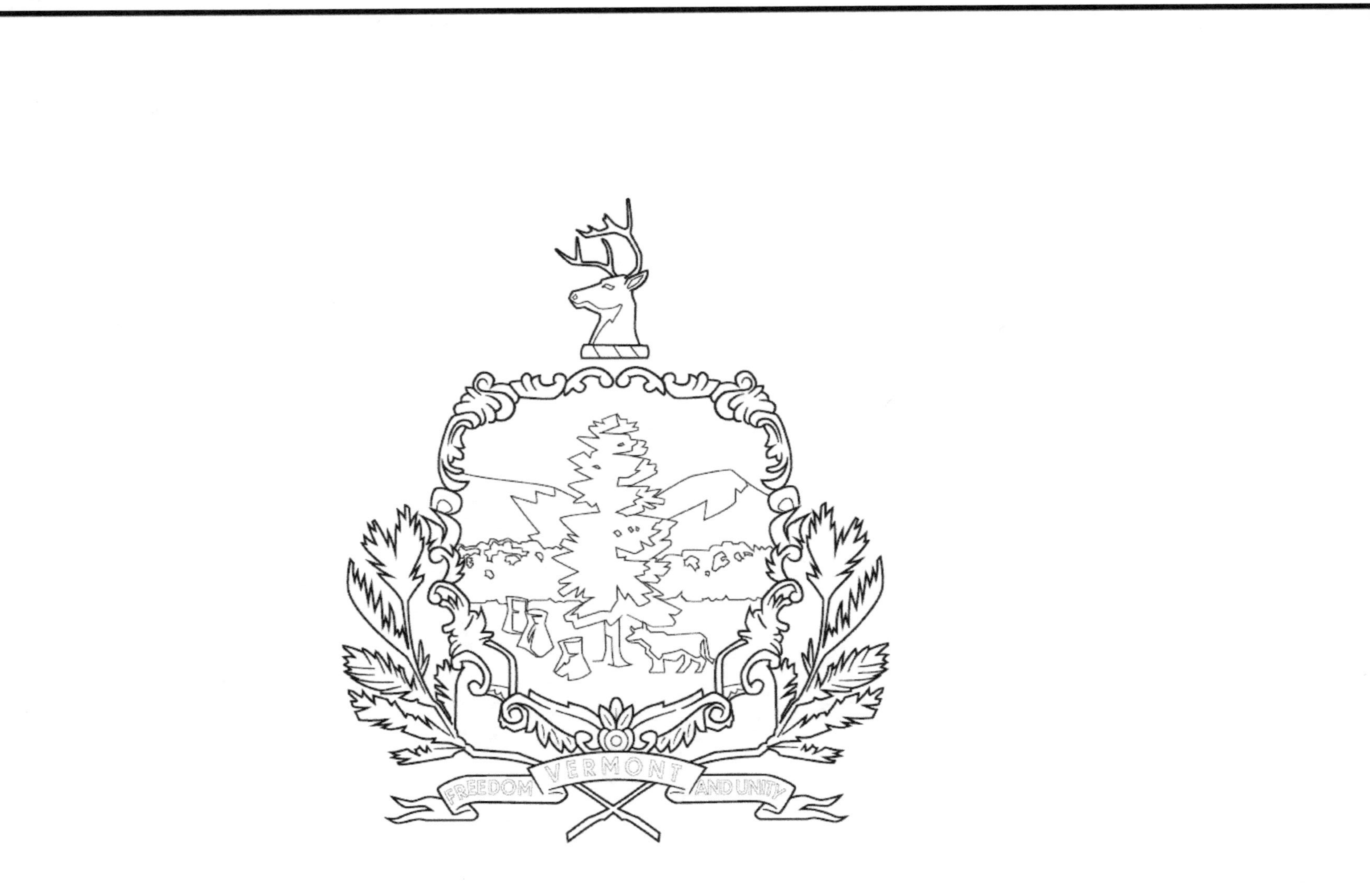

VERMONT

VIRGINIA
SIC SEMPER TYRANNIS

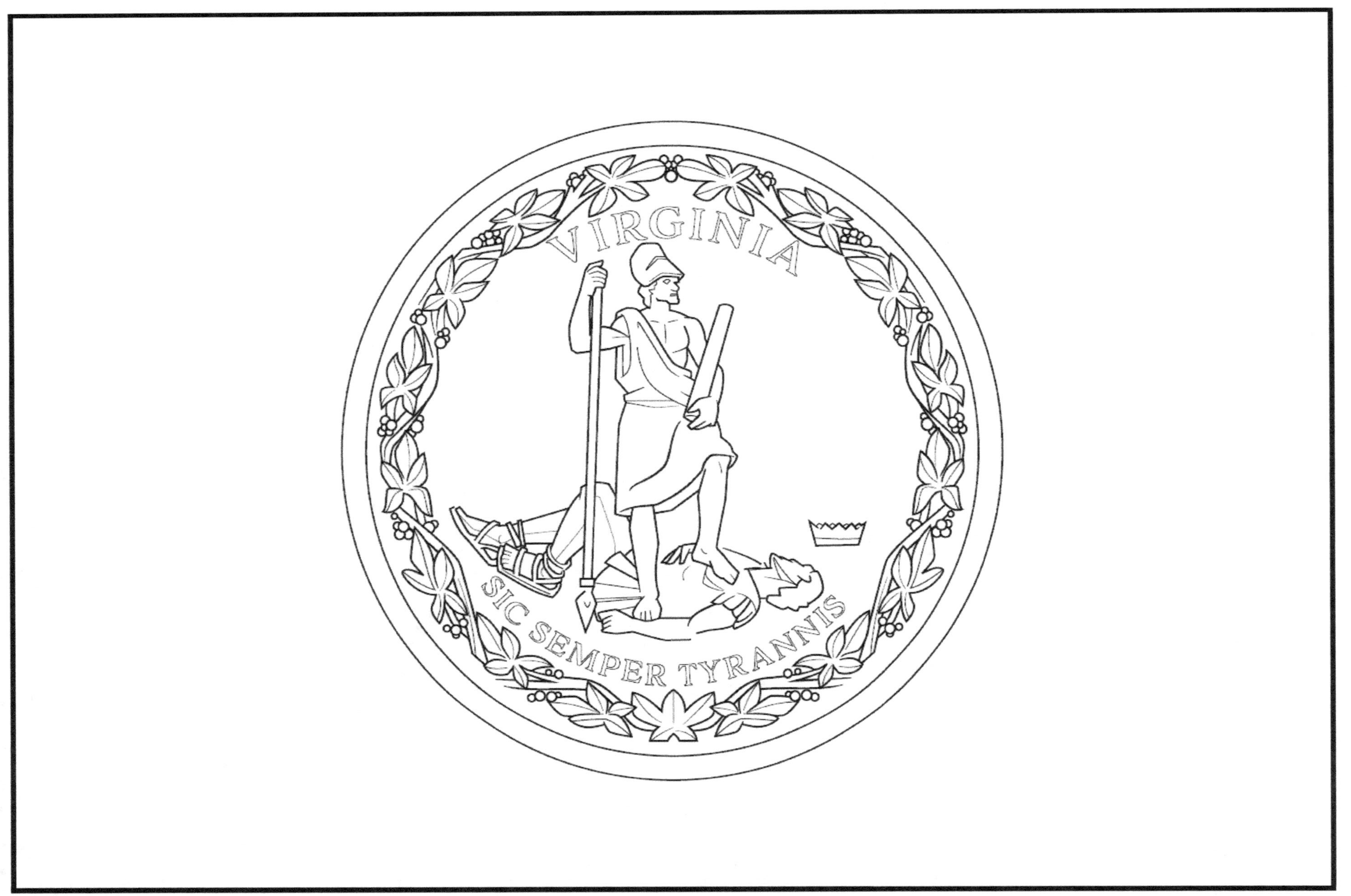

VIRGINIA

THE SEAL OF THE STATE OF WASHINGTON 1889

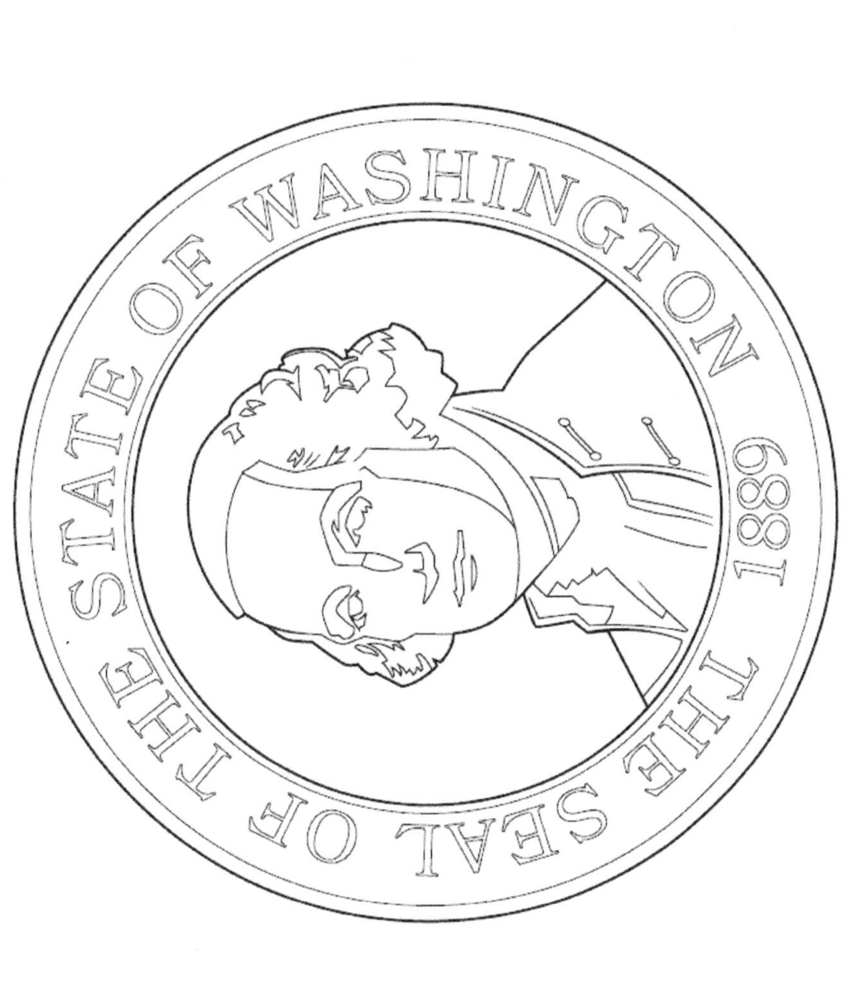

WASHINGTON

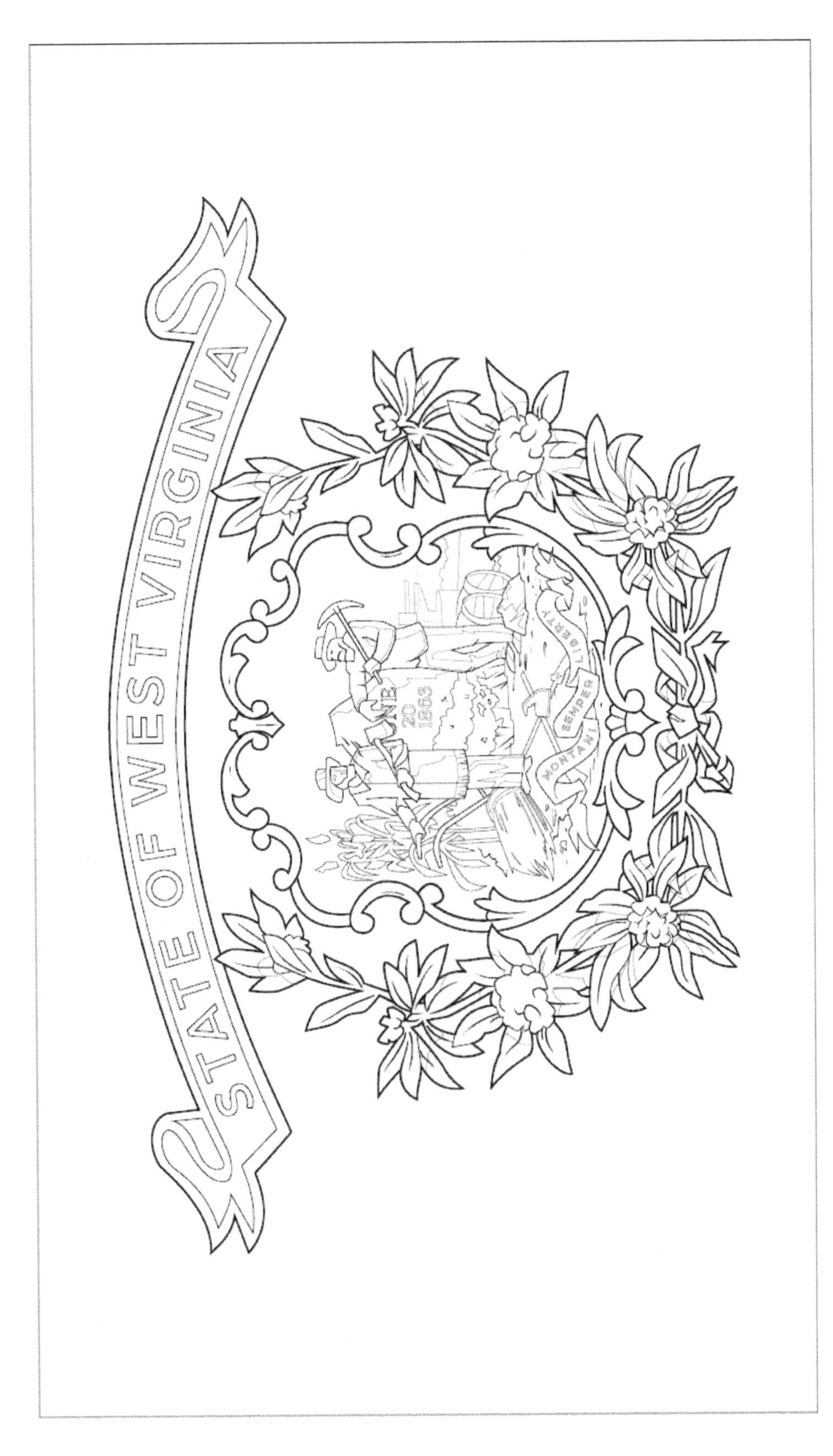

WEST VIRGINIA

 COLOR THE US: FLAG EDITION

WISCONSIN
FORWARD
E PLURIBUS UNUM
1848

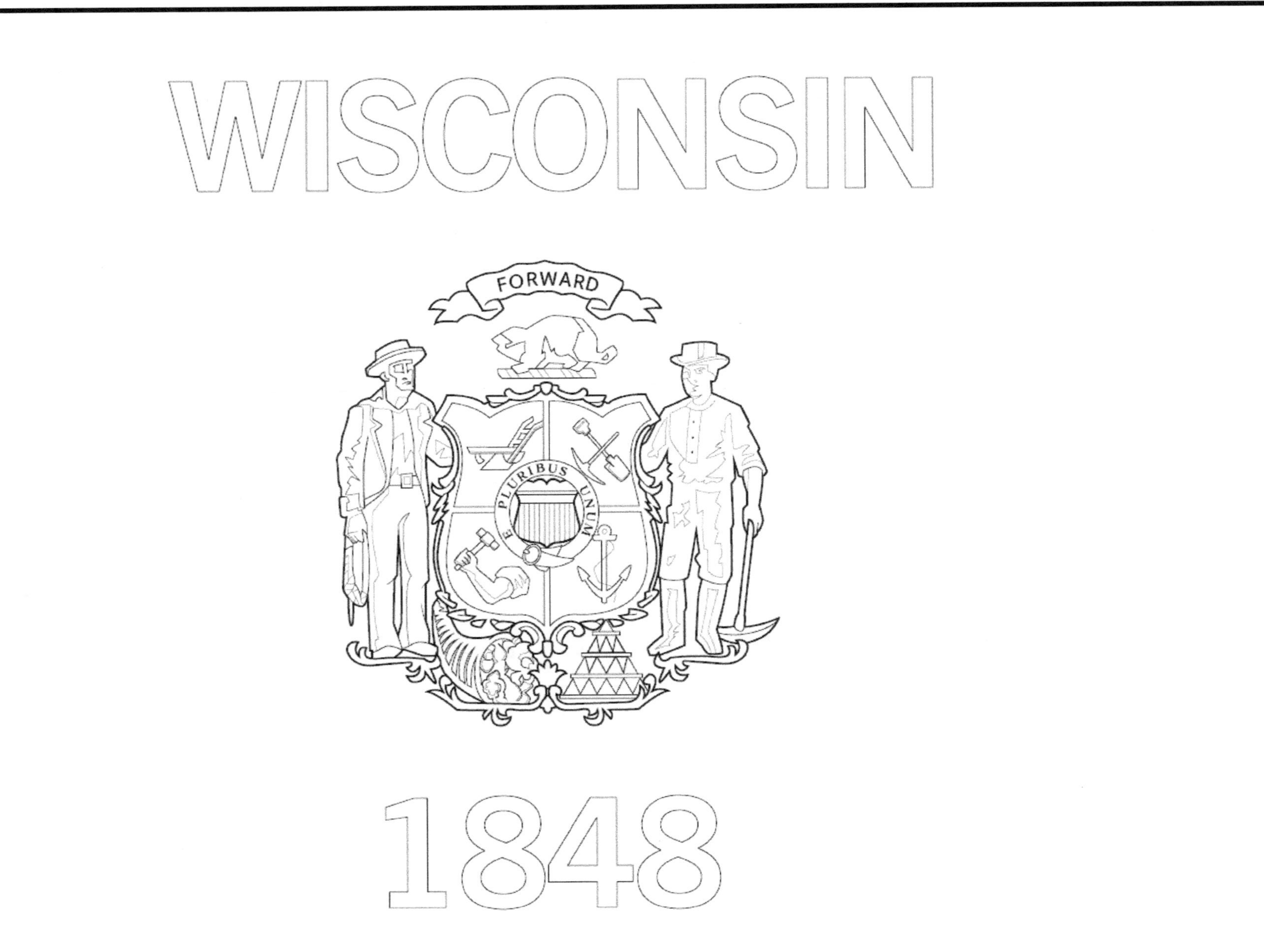

WISCONSIN

GREAT SEAL OF THE STATE OF WYOMING
EQUAL RIGHTS
LIVESTOCK
MINES
GRAIN
OIL

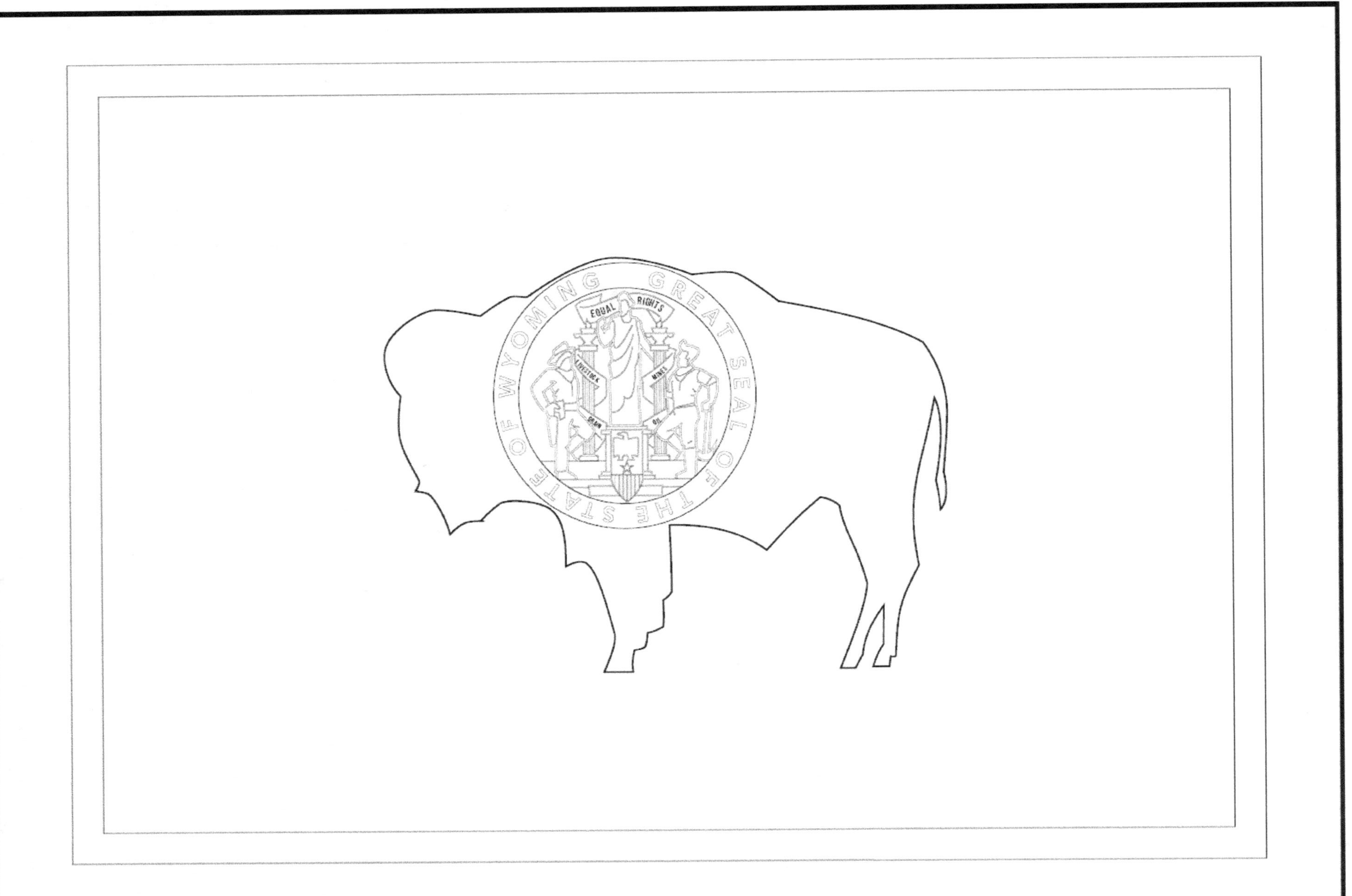

WYOMING

THE UNITED STATES OF AMERICA